THE BRIDES OF ENDERBY

Illustrated by Derek Crowe

RALPH TOWNLEY

THE BRIDES OF ENDERBY

A Lincolnshire Childhood

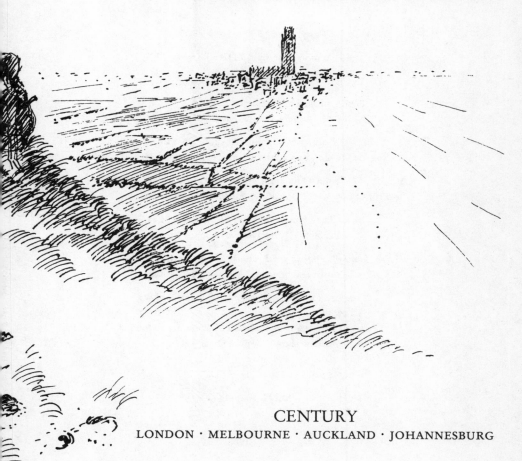

CENTURY

LONDON · MELBOURNE · AUCKLAND · JOHANNESBURG

By the same author:

THE UNITED NATIONS: A VIEW FROM WITHIN
THE EVOLUTION OF INTERNATIONAL INSTITUTIONS
(with others, D. E. T. Luard ed.)
A WORD OR TWO BEFORE YOU GO
(with Dr B. B. Waddy, co-author)

MADAM, I'M ADAM, a new version of ADAMUS EXUL
a play of Hugo Grotius, pub. 1601

First published in 1988 by Century Hutchinson Ltd
62–65 Chandos Place London WC2N 4NW

Century Hutchinson Australia Pty Ltd,
PO Box 496, 16–22 Church Street, Hawthorn, Victoria 3122, Australia

Century Hutchinson New Zealand Limited,
PO Box 40–086, Glenfield, Auckland 10, New Zealand

Century Hutchinson South Africa (Pty) Ltd,
PO Box 337, Bergvlei, 2012 South Africa

Typeset by Deltatype Lecru, Ellesmere Port, Cheshire
Printed and bound by Mackays of Chatham

British Library Cataloguing in Publication Data
Townley, Ralph
    The brides of Enderby : a Lincolnshire childhood.
    1. Lincolnshire——Social life and customs
    I. Title
    942.5'3083'0924   DA670.L7

ISBN 0–7126–1840–6

FOR

CHRISTOPHER AND

MIRANDA

Acknowledgements

To Derek Crowe, whose illustrations enliven the text, and Victoria Huxley, Editorial Director, and Sophie Jebb, her assistant, whose constant care and consideration made the publication of this book such a pleasure, I extend my warmest thanks.

Grateful acknowledgement is also made to Penguin Books Ltd for permission to reproduce an extract from *The Agricola and The Germania* by Tacitus, translated by H. Mattingly (Penguin Classics, 1948).

CONTENTS

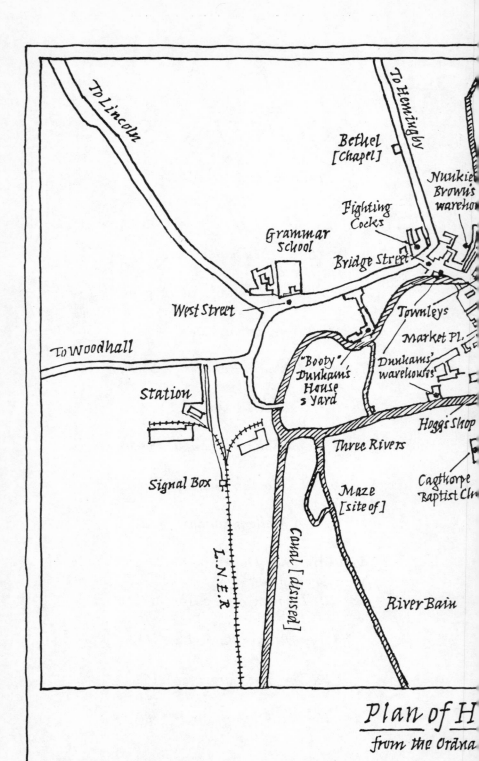

To Lincoln

To Hemingby

Bethel
[Chapel]

Nuukie
Brown's
warehou...

Fighting
Cocks

Grammar
School

Bridge Street

West Street

Townleys

Market Pl.

To Woodhall

"Booty"
Dunham's
House
s Yard

Dunhams'
warehouse's

Station

Hogg's Shop

Signal Box

Three Rivers

Maze
[site of]

Cagthorpe
Baptist Ch...

L.N.E.R.

Canal [disused]

River Bain

Plan of H

from the Ordna...

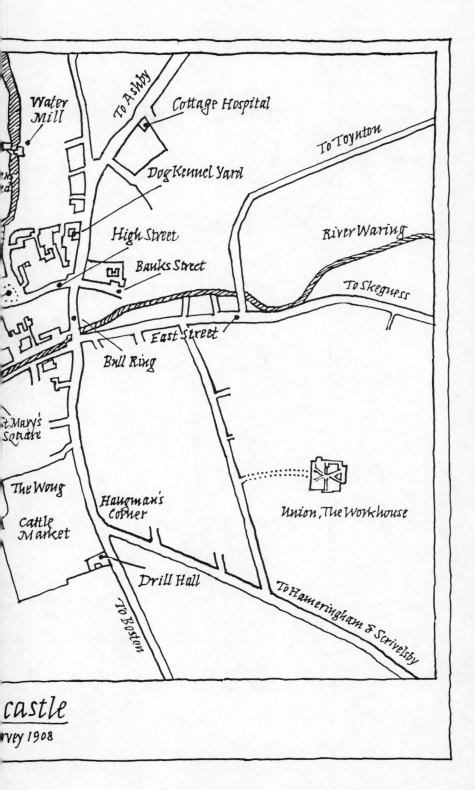

Water
Mill

To Ashby

Cottage Hospital

To Toynton

Dog Kennel Yard

River Waring

High Street

Banks Street

To Skegness

East Street

Bull Ring

St. Mary's
Square

The Woug

Hangman's
Corner

Union, The Workhouse

Cattle
Market

Drill Hall

To Boston

To Hameringham & Scrivelsby

castle

rvey 1908

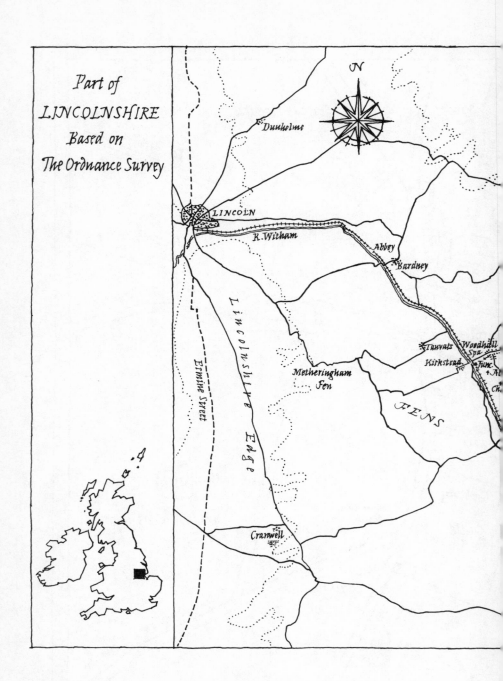

Part of
LINCOLNSHIRE
Based on
The Ordnance Survey

N

Dunholme

LINCOLN

R. Witham

Abbey

Bardney

Tawats

Woodhall
Spa

Kirkstead

Junc.

Metheringham
Fen

FENS

Lincolnshire Edge

Ermine Street

Cranwell

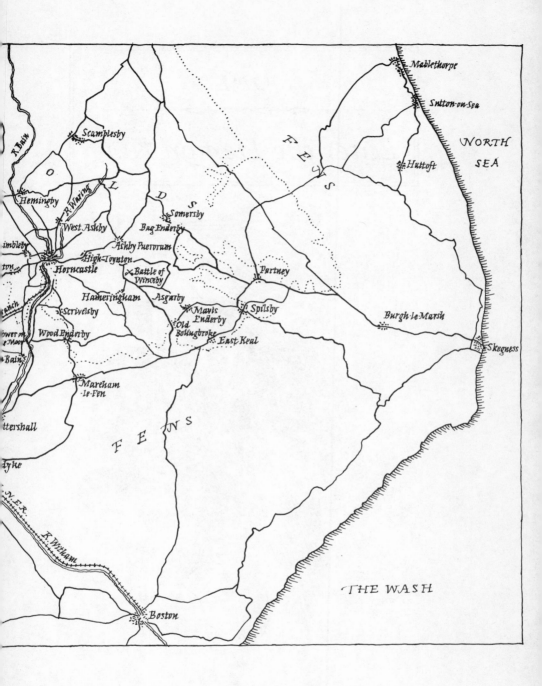

... looked just like
the Demon King

*T*he prince flung off his fencing mask with a gesture of exaggerated disdain, his great, ginger eyebrows curling up as malevolently as his moustaches. He waited for what seemed a lifetime, gathering his accumulated exasperation into a barely controlled snarl of frustration: 'Your weapon is a pen with which you write, so write, write. . . .' He tapped his foot – encased in one of those flashy, white and tan pointed shoes – and, with a supreme effort added, 'now, show your penmanship . . . gracefully, elegantly!'

The prince turned to the old rattan reclining chair that all summer long sat under the sycamore tree and was regarded by us children as his private preserve. Rummaging in his Norfolk jacket for a box of Swan Vestas, he relit his cigar, rolling it between his fingers until the tip glowed a dull red. He took a couple of puffs, picked up his mask and placed it on top of his head with the white bib pointing at me. Then, taking up his foil, he looked critically at me for a moment and said, 'Once more, on guard!' And with a gentle tap at the back of his mask with his left hand he fell into the on-guard position just as the mask slipped into place – a gesture that I had spent weeks trying, but failing, to emulate. The prince continued to puff on his cheroot and through the mesh of the mask the Havana smoke filtered, forming a halo round his head. I shouted with delight, for he looked just like the Demon King in the Christmas pantomime blowing smoke out of his ears as he rose through the trap door in the stage.

Then, in a voice slightly muffled by both mask and cigar, more kindly this time, the prince exhorted me: 'Write, Juggins, as if you were writing to your fiancée!' Trying to ply my foil as a pen with which I wrote finely and with grace was one thing, but being adjured, as a twelve-year-old schoolboy, to fence as if I were writing to my girl required a stretch of the imagination that, as yet, was beyond my reach. But I knew that the prince was not really angry, for when he got 'whacky', as my father put it, he would swear horribly in Turkish. My father never swore in any language.

With my flat feet floundering and all the rest of me hot and stiff inside the new jacket and breeches the prince had bought for me, I was as relentless as he. My one ambition at the time was to be a champion foil fencer; if Winston Churchill could, so could I, for he too had been an ungainly boy. The only fly in the ointment was that the prince regarded the foil as a lady's toy and the sabre the only weapon worth mastering. Reluctantly, therefore, he taught me foil – and with an exacting discipline, learnt first during his boyhood in Russia and later in Budapest, where he had lived precariously for a while as a *garçon de salle*, or attendant, in the academy of Santelli, then the greatest fencing master in all Europe.

I used to think that the annual visit of the prince went unheralded. His arrival came always as a tumultuous surprise. Summoned, so we were told, by a mysterious telegram, my father would have the governess cart harnessed or, in later years, the car brought round and off he would go to the railway station.

For whom was the occasion? With two exceptions, my father was known never to meet guests from trains. One such was my father's favourite sister, Florence. He insisted, however, that he meet her not at the local halt, but in Lincoln. Throughout his life my father was exacting in matters of not only his own dress, but also that of members of his family. Never flannels and an odd jacket, always a suit; never a soft collar, always a starched one. He had a horror of brown boots and hair lotion. I could never quite understand what sartorial solecism was committed by Aunt Florrie, however.

'I shall meet her,' my father would inform my mother waving a letter at the breakfast table, 'and take her to Mawer and Collingham, for she is bound to arrive wearing a blouse and skirt.'

He referred to the county tailor and outfitter where we all shopped, possibly because of Quaker connexions, and where my father's annual suit was made. What was wrong with a blouse and skirt, I wondered? My father found them *de trop* and none of his womenfolk ever wore them. So, as the local train from Nottingham puffed into St Mark's Station, my father was waiting on the platform ready to whisk Aunt Florrie off to Mawer and Collingham from where she emerged in a

... on the offside of the motor car we all stood in a row

new dress, with a box of additional ones for her stay, as well as a paper bag presumably containing the offending garments in which she had arrived. But there were no advance preparations of this kind, so it must be the prince who was coming.

Towards evening, after a fever of waiting, the cart – or the motor car – would turn into the yard. We all stood well back as my father's driving was, to say the least, somewhat impressionistic, and he needed a safety margin in case he forgot where to find the brake.

The crunch on the gravel was the music of the spheres. We stood entranced. Belton, my father's man, drew himself to attention. His daughter, Kathleen, waited shyly behind. Tommy, the yardman, held the horse's head or stood by the radiator on the nearside as if the bonnet had a bridle. George, the baker, appeared in his apron at the top of the granary steps wiping his hands, joined by Mrs Blades, our washerwoman, who had been up there airing laundry and having a bit of a gossip. Others who gathered included Hogg, the cobbler, on his way home to his tea, the one-legged upholsterer from the top warehouse and the Russian wife of the gunsmith in the Market Place, who made a little bob as the prince stepped down.

On the offside of the motor car we all stood in a row. For the boys, a bone-crushing handshake as the prince exclaimed at how we had all grown. First Frank, powerfully built, shy to the point of being sheepish. Then Muriel and Jane, my two sisters, standing together, their gypsy-black hair braided for the occasion in long pigtails. They knew it pleased the prince, for it reminded him of the home he would never see again. Normally their plaits were wound round their heads, and I once injured myself when very small trying to drive their hairpins into my head, for it seemed to me, watching them do their hair of a morning, that as *they* could do this with impunity, why could not I?

Frank, big and strong, dark-visaged and always gentle, he being the eldest was greeted with grave courtesy. I was all agog on one of the prince's earliest remembered visits, probably the same year I made my painful attempt to emulate my sisters with the hairpins, to have Frank blow up his muscles. I never tired of his doing it. With a mind that loved things mechanical, when he was as small as I was then, he had been mesmerized by Mrs Blades' sewing machine driven by a treadle. While her attention was taken elsewhere, Frank had put his hand under the needle, pushed the treadle with his foot and stitched his index finger. The scar was about a quarter of an inch long and he showed me how by blowing in it he could inflate his muscles. This he did to my delight and then he let me press my thumb on the scar to keep in the air. Slowly, as I lifted my thumb, the air escaped with a hiss and his muscles deflated. It seemed to me of no consequence that the sound of escaping air came from somewhere above my head.

There was always some incident of this kind that I wanted to share with our visitor, but the ritual of arrival was neither to be disturbed nor hurried. Turning to my other brother Harold, he enquired after his cricket or his tennis. The family's sportsman, Harold had the diffidence of the natural athlete and would roll his eyes under his cap that always seemed a mort small for him, deprecating his own performance but praising that of his team. My turn came next. My hair was ruffled and I was picked up and swung high over the prince's head and down his back. Then with a quick change of his grip he pulled my wrists through under his long legs, so that I landed on my feet, slightly dazed, on the spot where I had been standing.

Then to Belton, whom he kissed gently on his grizzled cheeks, enquiring after his health. The prince shook hands with Kathleen and asked after her mother. He patted Tommy on the back and waved a greeting to George and Mrs Blades and the one-legged upholsterer. Finally the prince, catching sight of the gunsmith's wife, strode over and took her hands in his while they conversed quietly in Russian. Tears ran down her broad, Slav cheeks. (She had been born in St Petersburg. I do remember once asking her to describe the city on the Neva, and asked if she had seen the French Impressionists there. She looked puzzled, then laughed and said that the Hermitage was, in her childhood, a palace from which the huge and terrifying Cossack soldiers drove children away as they crept forward on starlit, ice-cold evenings to watch the guests alight from their carriages.)

The moment then came for which we had all waited. My mother came to the door and stepped down. The prince doffed his broad-brimmed hat and placed it over his heart. We stood enraptured and silently all mouthed the magic incantation: 'And how is the lady of the house?' Thereupon he bent very low and kissed my mother on her right cheek, then on her left and then again on her right. We repeated, wordlessly, the response, 'Dear Vanya, how you always smell of cough medicine and violets!' The moment was one of stillness and enchantment.

Thus the arrival ended. No longer transfixed, we sprang to grab his traps, boxes and bundles and scurried with them up to the old nursery which was to be his home for the next two months. Then we filed down to the evening meal, leaving the prince to replenish himself with 'cough medicine' and refresh himself with toilet water. Usually a guest was asked to say grace but, on these occasions, my father sought a somewhat perfunctory blessing. We watched as the prince crossed himself. I remember with a shock of recollection, as if looking in an old glass, when first I attended a Catholic Mass seeing people crossing themselves from left to right only ever having seen the prince at table cross himself Orthodox fashion the other way round.

We fell on our food: stuffed chine, pork pie and huge, musky-smelling tomatoes from the conservatory. In rare silence, and with rapidly diminishing patience, we listened while the grown-ups exchanged news. Although he was my father's friend, my mother's admirer and someone who was acquainted with her well before I was born, somehow we knew that he really belonged to us children. He was our Demon King, who opened up new vistas of excitement with every puff of his cigar. He was for my sisters their dancing partner; for my brothers their tutor and counsellor; for me he was chief botanist, fencing master, president of the Old Rasputin Restoration Society (I was the only other officer of it) and, in due course, honorary colonel of the Foreign Legion.

Our impatience had, however, a more immediate cause. We had seen the boxes which, later in the evening, would be brought downstairs to the drawing room. There, slowly, with exasperating slowness, the contents were distributed. Books for my father; a stole for my mother; long, sleeveless coats, called sarafans, for my sisters; a rotating star map for Frank; a complicated chest expander for Harold; and for me, (I still have them) *kovshi*, or gaily painted wooden spoons, and a *kvass*, a wooden bowl for soup or porridge. When I joined the Foreign Legion there was a Bowie knife with a compass set in the horn (or was it bone?) handle. The year I went away to school he brought the fencing uniform from Paris complete with glove, elbow guard, stockings and shoes.

The presents were treasured, for they *were* treasures, and used because they were so practical. Not all, however. One year Muriel and Jane were given *kokoshniki* – those tall, embroidered headdresses Russian girls would wear on high days and holidays. Surreptitiously, they were spirited away to join a great collection of garments in the dressing-up cupboard. This was a huge linen press set aside for our costumes and garments unsuitable for normal wear but heaven to rummage through when some masquerade was to be performed, usually led by Muriel and Harold. Once the prince, still very thin from a bout of fever he had suffered in the Congo, had brought my mother a plain ivory bracelet. It startled her, and after a brusque 'Thank you, Vanya dear,' the box was handed to Kathleen with the quite peremptory request that it be put away immediately in my mother's bedroom. Many years later I asked why she had not only never worn it, but never touched it. 'Anthrax,' she said abruptly. And the subject was closed.

As soon as I could, I dragged the prince to the attic where, in the large central area which had become our playroom, I would show him what I had added to my store since his last visit. An Indian war bonnet sent for Christmas from Calgary, where my Uncle Jack was bank manager; an electric shock machine, discarded as unsatisfactory for the treatment of rheumatism, given me by Belton who worked occasionally in the cottage hospital garden; the sets of lead soldiers: mounted Spahis, charging Zulus, staunch Highlanders, crawling Indian braves and, one year, a field gun. But, most beautiful of all, was the plywood main-line railway station made for me by one of my brothers' friends. It took four Hornby railway tracks, had two platforms and a working clock. The walls were festooned with bill boards advertising the products sold and services provided by the different branches of my family.

So summer began. With the windows wide open to catch the breeze, night sounds became more audible. First to be heard was the chant of crickets in the granary. Later, the slap of the moorhen's wings on the water below the bridge punctuated the quick ripple of the river as it ran over the pebbles in the stream above the house. One night a week was always disturbed by the lowing of the beasts, out at the back, being starved as they were destined for slaughter on the morrow. Then as the darkness thinned, the click of the bakehouse door sneck as George arrived to light the great 'flash' oven. The scrape of his broad shovel as he stoked the furnace was the last sound I heard as I slipped into sleep again, snuggling into the blankets in the dawn chill, to awaken to the clank of approaching copper cans of hot water for washing and shaving, and the smell of freshly baked bread, frying bacon and grilled pork sausages. Already

19

... I dragged the prince to the attic

the reflection of the sunlight on the river was dappling the ceiling golden.

The day that had begun at dawn with the arrival of the head baker was governed and ordered until midnight by the demands and occasional temperamental quirks of the ancient bake-oven. Occupying nearly half the space of the bakehouse, it was fifty or more feet in diameter, with a flagstone floor and shallow-domed, quoined brick roof. Above it lay the granaries, underneath ran a small railway and to the right stood, topped by a giant water-boiler, the open-backed furnace leading into the oven itself. The bake-oven was a century old by the time I was born, and already something of a curiosity. It was known technically as a flash oven because of the method of its firing.

George would stoke the furnace with a quick-burning coal, the flames from which spread across the oven as more fuel was shovelled in. Peeking through the glory-hole in the oven door, George could judge unerringly from the red glow of the brick lining exactly when the right temperature had been reached. From the moment he took his decision speed was of the essence. The double doors of the furnace were flipped open and, with a long iron hook, the coals raked down into the ashpit beneath in a great shower of sparks and a cascade of gleaming clinkers and red-hot cinders. Slamming the door shut, George would reach for his flail. This was a thirty-foot ash pole secured at one end to five feet or so of heavy chain, to which was hooked a frequently replaced flour sack. This was soaked in a bucket of hot water, the oven door flung open wide and the flail plunged, rattling and spitting, on the flagstones into the ash-strewn depths of the oven. With a clever flick of the wrists, George would set the flail in motion, swirling it around the oven floor in a circular movement. As the speed increased the flail became invisible in the maelstrom of ash and cinders which were stirred up to join the smoke already hanging thick from the raked coals. Just as suddenly, the clank of the chain and the hiss of the wet sacking would cease; the flail was withdrawn and the oven door slammed shut. The final step in the firing process was to pull out the long flange of the damper. This opened the flue, and immediately up the

21

chimney shot ash, dust, cinders, smoke, in fact anything that would not leave the oven bright, hot and clean for the day's baking.

Meanwhile, with the covers taken off the bread bins, the yeast had begun to work in the dough. George and his assistants, who had by now arrived for the day, would knead the dough with their arms plunged deep into the floury mass. When it was ready and beginning to rise rapidly it would be lifted on to the bin tops. Still rising, it would be cut, weighed, moulded and popped into the waiting, freshly greased bread tins. These were laid out on wooden racks on the 'proving' wagon that trundled out on rails from the prover under the oven. Weighed down with hundreds of bread tins, the wagon would rumble back into its cavern where the dough would continue to rise.

When George decided that it was proved and ready, the batch would be run out and transferred to the oven. Everyone had to move fast, for the heat must be conserved. He would then take down from its overhead rack the peel, or long shovel (from, I suppose, the French *pelle*). He would slide it over the flagstones into the oven, conveying six bread tins at a time. Thus hundreds of loaves could be shot into the oven in a matter of minutes, the last ones almost nestling against the oven door. The oven would be closed, the peel returned to its place, the bins scraped down, the implements scrubbed and drained, and then everyone would go to his breakfast.

An hour later, when the bread was ready, work would be resumed. Protective sacks would be spread on the bins to keep them clean. Down would come the peel again, the door of the oven would be flung open and George would carefully draw out the freshly baked loaves, all browned and crusty. While he rested the peel on the oven sill, willing hands encased in thick mitts would snatch up the tins and spill them on to the bin tops. This too had to be a swift process in order to preserve the oven's heat – for it would be used throughout the day. While it was still 'sharp' or fast, buns, teacakes, rolls and other bread doughs were baked. These were followed by pastries, parkins and the ever popular Bakewell tarts. In the afternoon a slower oven absorbed the heavy Lincolnshire plum bread, pork pies and large cakes.

Towards evening the slow-baking, largest fruit cakes and festive cakes were put in the oven by the confectioners, who often preferred to work late. Finally, in the spaces left vacant by the cakes, the great hams for which my family were noted would bake gently until after midnight. Thus the oven's day and ours ended, with crickets chirping and big, black beetles rustling as they emerged from the distant recesses of the prover to repossess their territory. Then all would be silence until in the early hours the unmistakable click of the bakehouse latch would announce the start of a new day.

Once the prince had arrived the only cloud in the sky was that he had to be shared. Frank occupied him with machinery, motor cars and motorbikes; Harold with cricket; Jane with swimming, while Muriel needed a partner for tennis or a companion for riding. This last one could never grudge, for a fall that had led to what had seemed at first a slight injury, had well nigh crippled her. My father, for some unknown reason, had called Muriel after her namesake in Dinah Craik's *John Halifax, Gentleman*. It is true that that Victorian novelist had chosen Tewkesbury, my father's and grandfather's birthplace, as the setting for Norton-bury in the novel. The Abbey Mill where the Quaker, Abel Fletcher, made a handsome living and The Bell, where he lived, were a stone's throw from my father's medieval home – but, why Muriel? Poor Muriel of the novel, she lived a miserable existence and her suffering was Dickensian in its selflessness and duration. Which is worse for a child to contemplate, the reality of suffering or its fictionalized version? Reading this appalling piece of Victorian sentimentality deepened in me at quite an early age the intensity of compassion and sense of helplessness when witnessing the struggle over her handicap of the real Muriel.

It was not always a question of sharing, though. Sometimes the absence of the prince was part of a punishment. A child who is beaten daily probably thinks nothing of it. The spoiled brat, who is thrashed once or twice in his childhood retains an indelible memory of the event. My father only administered severe punishment if he found out that one of his children had

been discovered mimicking or deriding the infirmity of others. Nunkie Brown, recluse, sometime chauffeur and bicycle mender, having a hare-lip and lacking a roof to his mouth, was a tempting subject for our histrionic skills.

I exercised mine just once too often and was taken in quaking dread to the place of execution in the bottom warehouse. It was so chosen, I had once been told by Jane in hushed tones, as the building where our screams would be muffled and least heard by others. To add insult to anticipated injury, the bottom ware-house, as it looked over the water steps, was my special hangout and it was awful to see it assume a new, threatening and sinister aspect. Added to this humiliation was the invoking of one of our Quaker 'saints', namely John Woolman, the early eighteenth-

... *usually started with walking the town*

century Philadelphian tailor and mystic, much admired by father. As my backside reddened he kept time with his rod of chastisement by chanting from Woolman's *Journal*:

Enjoy NOT, that which HARDens thy HEART!

The aftermath was even more painful for, being a pariah, I was shunned by all, including the prince; but, happily, not for long. Our joint perambulations usually started with walking the town, noting small changes – just as children coming home after an interval away ritualistically walk through every room in the house as if re-establishing territorial rights. But in Horncastle, our small market town remote in the Lincolnshire Wolds, there were few changes to be seen. We would go through the Fighting Cocks innyard, skirting the site of the old cockpit, and down past the little tin-roofed Bethel where the Beltons went to chapel. Soon we would reach open country as far as the watermill on the river Bain that my grandfather's great-grandfather had built in the eighteenth century. The combination of stone, wood and water in a rural setting restored and refreshed his spirit and, for this reason perhaps, the prince always made the mill the terminal point of the first of our walks. So back we would stroll, skirting the Roman wall, past the hangman's shop, across the Market Place and along streets whose houses displayed Georgian fanlights and, in alcoves, small ornate decorations and embellishments.

Outings were our speciality: to the seaside on fine Sundays, to the moors on Wednesdays – early closing day – and, in the long summer evenings, to the wolds. But many of these trips too were for business, and I was often left to wait for my father and the prince while they completed their deals in corn or negotiated the wool clip. Journeys for the wool clip would be made in the morning when the mist still lay thick on the wold bottoms. The fleeces in each farm had to be sorted, counted and checked before being baled. Those of old tups and dead sheep were flung aside (with a reproachful look at the farmer), and cotts piled separately. Cotts were matted fleeces that the machines in Bradford were not strong enough to comb out and were paid at a lower price.

My special task, for which I was paid a penny a pound, was to sweep up the barn and bag the scag ends. These were the wool clippings from around the sheep's hindquarters usually clotted with droppings. The smell of ammonia was over-powering but not unpleasant. And, when the dung was washed off the scags, the wool fetched a modest but worthwhile price. As the fragments could not be combed and spun, scag ends were used almost exclusively for mattress stuffing.

Sometimes, if the wool clip was a large one, we would stay to midday dinner with the farmer, who usually fed us a meal of fat ham, pickled onions and homemade chutney. Afterwards, I would join Tommy the yardman who was asleep in the hedge, having eaten his 'baggin' out of doors or in a stable. We would wander down the lane from the farm and he would pick out the wild flowers, the names of which most amused him: old man's beard, lady's smock, shepherd's purse, fat-hen, fleabane and poor man's weather-glass.

Later would come the corn harvest. We raced through the sheaves to knobble rabbits as the reaper reduced the square into which they had retreated and leaped and shouted under the guns standing at four corners of the field. The prince had one corner and my father another, Uncle Tommy the third. Occasionally a hare would leap by. Uncle Tommy, a very good shot, would always bring it down. My father and the prince never fired at them. Once I asked why. 'Never shoot at a hare, Boy,' the prince explained, 'for if you only wing it it screams like a wounded man.' He then fell silent as if in recollection. I have never shot a hare.

Best of all, possibly because no work was expected of me, were the summer evening expeditions up the wolds. My father and the prince had a particular affection for East Keal, where the chalk hills fell away abruptly to the fens. From there we could look east to the distant, shining sea and south-west to watch the sun go down behind Boston Stump – the great tower of St Botolph's, which surmounted by its magnificent lantern top-storey, dominated the fenland and provided a beacon for sailors entering the Wash.

On such evenings Belton would take his ferret to find a rabbit. Afterwards I always had to force myself to look at the ferret curled up against his chest with the blood of its latest kill still on its snout. My sisters would bicycle up to join us. My father and the prince would unlace their boots, discard their jackets and waistcoats and brace themselves for a bout of wrestling. Somewhere in his youth my father had been apprenticed in the north, in Westmoreland, where he learned Fell wrestling – wherein the opponents lock their arms around one another and throws have to be made by foot, leg or hip as the hand grip must not be broken. Fell wrestling, as its name implies, took place on the short, sheep-nibbled grass of the fellside, and our Keal hill was perfect for this, being grassy and steep. (Doctor Johnson, in spite of his bulk, had once amazed his Langton friends by rolling down it.) Stretching beyond us were green fields and puff-ball clouds: a Peter de Wint landscape.

The prince was tall and fairly agile, but was never a match for my father who was not only nimble but brawny. Soon they would lie gasping on their backs on the grass and listen to the bell-ringers practising in Boston Stump. You could just hear the peal across the fens if the wind was right. The prince loved bells and would tell us stories – only half-believed – of a bell, which having been rung as a signal to mutiny against Catherine the Great, had had its clapper removed for punishment. In Rostov on the river Don, said the prince, there was a bell that could be heard twenty miles away.

That was considerably further than the Boston bells carried, but like all church bells from the tenth century onwards, they were used to warn as well as to summon. Boston, indeed, had its own special peal to warn townfolk and surrounding fen dwellers of imminent danger – from pirates seen approaching the Wash, from flood waters bursting open the sluice gates or high tides breaching the coastal dykes. Just north of Keal, beyond the raised castle mound of Old Bolingbroke, the road winds through the wold village of Mavis Enderby, whose womenfolk were celebrated in an earlier century when the bells were first hung. The warning peal was called 'The Brides of Enderby' and was immortalized by Jean Ingelow, a Victorian poetess very much in the same mould as Dinah Craik, in her poem 'The High Tide on the Coast of Lincolnshire, 1571':

> The old mayor climbed the belfry tower
> The ringers ran by two, by three;
> 'Pull, if ye never pulled before;
> Good ringers, pull your best,' quoth he.
> 'Play uppe, play uppe, O Boston bells!
> Ply all your changes, all your swells,
> Play uppe "The Brides of Enderby".'

The Boston bellringers sometimes practised the warning at the end of their mid-week change-ringing. Up on Keal hill one

Wednesday we stayed to listen. The prince moved down wind of us and lit a cheroot. My sisters plaited corn dollies from our gleanings. My father pulled on his boots. 'The mellow lin-lan-lone of evening bells', as Tennyson described them, came to us across the fenland. I remember feeling a disquieting, almost physical tug of the warning peal – or was it a summons? What did life hold that I was to be both cautioned and commanded? The bells rocked into stillness as we packed up our traps and made our way home to supper.

Such recollections of one's early years cannot help but be fragmented. They are like the clearings in the mist that rise from the fens or roll in from the sea to enshroud the wolds. Sounds fade, briars clutch and Jack o'Lanterns beguile. Perceptions of distance and direction are easily lost before the miasma breaks and the landscape is seen once more, if only fleetingly, with startling clarity.

... the Boston bellringers sometimes practised the warning

TWO

The Pleasant Land of Thermogene

The climate is objectionable, with its frequent rains and mists,
but there is no extreme cold. Their days are longer than is
normal in the Roman world. Crops are slow to ripen but quick
to grow, both facts due to one and the same cause, extreme
moistness of land and sky.   TACITUS: *Agricola*

*... secured by four safety pins
inside my clean Sunday shirt*

*T*hus Agricola found Britain in the first century AD. This description by Tacitus could certainly apply to Lincolnshire except for the statement that there is no extreme cold. Snow may lie on the northern sides of hedgerows until early June, and lambing time in the wolds is often hazardous. The north-easters howl straight down the North Sea directly from the Arctic tundra and across the unprotected hills. My mother loved this sharp, clear weather. It infused her with energy. Unhappily for me I could not share in this enthusiasm. 'Mark my words', the family doctor had warned her when I was a baby, 'every time that north-east wind blows, this child will cough!' I must have done my best to conform to this medical opinion for, at some date between the time of the prince's departure and early November – when fogs and mists were already very much in evidence – a thick, square wad of pink, camphorated wool would be secured by four safety-pins inside my clean Sunday shirt. There it would lodge, like Belton's ferret, until Saturday bath night, when it would be removed, matted and scratchy. In this way I wore a breastplate to guard me from the elements throughout the winter and spring until, at the end of May, I was released from the warming comfort of my thick wad of Thermogene.

It has often been said of Lincolnshire that it comprises ten per cent land and ninety per cent sky. Little known and not much visited, our county was made up of three distinct areas corresponding roughly to its three Ridings: Kesteven, Lindsey and Holland. The North Sea, the Wash and the Humber estuary formed its borders on the east, south and north, while on the west side flowed Shakespeare's 'smug and silver Trent'. Beyond that great river was Sherwood Forest, the Dukeries, heavy industry, large smoky towns and the coal pits, the grey-faced denizens of which were to make such a vivid impression on me in due course. Running parallel with the Trent ran the Roman road Ermine Street. Along Ermine Street the ill-fated Ninth Legion had tramped to its garrison at York, and it was the same road followed centuries later by Nicholas Nickleby, accompanied by Mr Squeers and his snivelling charges on top of the stage-coach.

Sheltered from the worst of the north-easters under a spur of the wolds and looking south to the fens stood our market town of Horncastle. Although many of the houses and shops boasted fine, eighteenth-century frontages, the red brick that crumbled but never seemed to weather looked always drab and depressing, a view shared by Daniel Defoe when he visited the wold market towns two hundred years before.

Four streets converged on the Bull Ring, once the town centre; the High Street led to the Market Place, across which my mother stated it took a Townley two hours to walk – it took her two minutes, but then she was not as 'gabby' as her menfolk. Its chief feature was an undistinguished, mock-gothic memorial subscribed to by an impoverished tenantry in dutiful memory of a by-no-means impoverished landlord who had gone to meet his Maker towards the close of the nineteenth century. The main streets and squares were linked by narrow, cobbled 'entries' or passageways just wide enough to take a hand cart, perhaps dating from medieval times, when Horncastle was an important market for the surrounding countryside. But the town's fame rested from the seventeenth century up until the 1930s on the Great August Horse Fair, which was reputed to be the largest horse fair in Europe. For descriptions of it in its heyday we must rely on that nineteenth-century traveller and observer of rural life George Borrow, in his book *The Romany Rye*. For where there are horses there are Romanies. There are also public houses, against which my puritan family inveighed – not always in vain: there were sixty odd in the town which, at the time I was born, had only three and a half thousand inhabitants. Enough inns in which to slake if not drown the thirst of the most vociferous horse coper.

Our house, with its Jacobean frontage marred by the addition of mid-Victorian shop windows, stood on the corner of Bridge Street between the bridge and the Market Place. Through it constantly flowed family, relatives, friends, servants, customers and tradespeople. It was comfortable and enfolding; if it had a shortcoming it was lack of privacy. But that would have been difficult to achieve, for my parents were hospitable and my mother's family of wold and fen farmers all congregated in our house on market days. Puffing on great pipes (except in my father's presence) they filled the kitchen and the downstairs sitting room with their talk of livestock prices and the weather (good or bad), drank endless cups of tea and waded through mountains of plum bread before clambering into their traps and trotting home. Uncle George from Asgardby, the only one of my mother's uncles my father cared for, usually had to be helped up into his trap at the close of market day. But the sober pony led him unerringly home to the remote farm in the wolds.

The life of the town mirrored that of the countryside. Seen through the eyes of the youngest child in the family, peering round the skirts and leggings of the grown-ups, it seemed harsh. Often toothless and rheumatic, their knuckles cracked and red with chilblains, the women looked older than their years. Widows abounded, for so many young men had not come back from the War; those that did seemed prematurely aged. Each day brought with it a reminder that life, if no longer short, was still brutish, and none was more poignant than Lady Day and Michaelmas. These two quarter-days, the twenty-fifth of March and the twenty-ninth of September, stood out in the farming year as the days on which farms changed hands, and labourers, no longer needed by old masters, moved to new. Thus two feast days of the Church were celebrated by a dismal and dreary procession of farm wagons with labourers and their families perched precariously on top of their meagre

... dismal and dreary procession

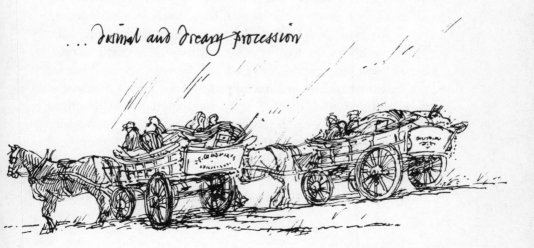

belongings being transported from the known to the un-known. Furthermore, it usually rained and instead of a tarpaulin to protect their bits and pieces, it was invariably the family feather bed that absorbed the downpour.

Such prosperity as the wold people enjoyed rested on the backs of the long-wooled Brocklesby sheep. *Wold* in Anglo-Saxon, according to my father's friend, 'Spider' Birkett, means 'wooded hill'. But the woods were replaced long ago by pasture for these same sheep. Since medieval times the wool clip has been the mainstay of conversation, and in Chaucer's day the staple was sent to Lincoln to be dyed the popular shade of green, a favourite among all who hunted or, as in the case of Robin Hood and his men, were hunted.

Farmhouses, barns and cottages nestled on the western slopes for, although these were less fertile than the reverse side, they were sheltered from the wind and in earlier times had provided concealment from the Danes and Norsemen. The wolds, of chalk and clay, unlike the older limestone, lacked good stone for building so that in both the wolds and fens the houses were built of the ubiquitous dull, red brick, although farm frontages were occasionally enlivened by Dutch gabling. In the wolds narrow lanes wound between deep hedgerows, in summer full of Queen Anne's lace and purple loosestrife and festooned with hay wisps caught by the sour blackthorn branches from passing wagons.

In the northern wolds the wink of Spurn Head Light beckoned us from across the Humber. Between it and the Donna Nook fens on our side of the estuary, vessels heading for Grimsby and Hull seemed, by some trick of the light, to be sailing in the sky. Along the coast southwards ran the fenlands, broadening out around the Wash into plains of rich alluvium, the celebrated Lincolnshire tulip fields. This level landscape, now drained and dyked, was dominated by tall, spired churches, some with broach steeples, others, like Boston, crowned with a great lantern top-storey. Boston Stump held sway in the south and, although on a clear day we had a distant prospect of Lincoln cathedral, in our imaginings we looked not westward for inspiration but eastward to the sea. Then, as

. . . occasionally enlivened by Dutch gabling

now, Dutch and Scandinavian influences persisted. We were
reminded of them when Baltic timber freighters unloaded at
Boston, or coal-burning Grimsby trawlers, blackening the sky
with their smokestacks, trudged home from trawling for cod in
the White Sea or drifting for herring on the Dogger Bank.

Close to the larger rivers this landscape was freakishly
patched together by bizarre peat hags and areas of blown sand.
There stood strange, abandoned, medieval hunting towers and
ghostly, ruined choirs of priories overgrown with heather,
gorse and bracken. Pinewoods grew dense on the moorland
edges. In them the forest paths, heavy with the resinous scents
of summer, led to silent and secluded clearings. On the west
side of the county the outer frontier of my consciousness was
Ermine Street, the old Roman road that ran along the sharp,
limestone cliff known as the Lincolnshire Edge. Beyond the
Edge was *terra incognita*, whose inhabitants we glimpsed
rarely except when, in crowded charabancs, they passed
through Horncastle on their way to seaside holidays at
Mablethorpe or Skegness.

What were we like, we Lincolnshire 'yeller-bellies'? The
name has stuck like the fenland mud that dried yellow on our
jackets and breeches. Perhaps that is its origin; but more likely

it comes from the buff waistcoats once worn by the Lincoln-shire regiment.

Our character and behaviour spring from the old Danelaw, the influence of which to my mind has persisted because of this relative isolation of the county from the rest of England. Under the Danelaw the land was not held by charter, but by the curious custom or testimony of the 'Wapentake'. At such gatherings the raising of spears and battle-axes (the 'weapon-take') was an act of public witness and confirmation of a man's rights. This bred in the people a strong sense of equality, independence and self-confidence – reflected in modern times by a pattern of yeoman rather than tenant farmers.

Unlike the old feudal lands to the south, Lincolnshire had no real squirearchy, a feature that occasioned comment a thousand years ago by the commissioners on their rounds compiling *The Domesday Book*. There were neither coal mines to provide the royalties nor large cities the urban ground rents to sustain great landowners. A small number of estates, few on a grand scale, did not bespeak great wealth and where there were landlords, rents were minimal or, in hard times, not

... derived from the heavy consumption of pork

charged at all. Most land was held in families, tenaciously, and made doubly secure by frequent intermarriage. Some genetic oddities resulted – and in this my mother's family was no exception – but more often the marriage of cousins led to infertility, which in its turn meant more concentrated land holdings.

In Lincolnshire the descendants of the Danish and Norse settlers were short, solid and powerful in build. They frequently retained the trait of thick, reddish-black hair. In fact, after the green of the countryside, red seemed to be the dominant colour of my childhood: the dark-red poll or hornless cattle, dull, red brick houses, the red blazers of the local grammar school, and above all, our own red countenances, which a less friendly observer might have termed choleric. If they were, our high colour must have been derived from the heavy consumption of pork. Many households, mine included, would think nothing of eating pork four times a day: pie or bacon for breakfast, cold ham at midday, sausages at high tea and stuffed chine or chitterlings for supper.

A race of John Bulls, bluff, genial and kindly of manner, happy in a stable society – not noticing that it was also static – envying no one and always glad to return home from where wars or other duties might have taken them. Hardened by the harsh and arid winds of puritanism, however, the bluff could quickly become gruff, and good humour degenerate into a sardonic mirthlessness which could be abrasive. Sometimes it was not easy to determine how far humour went before solemnity intervened, as on a tombstone in the churchyard of Boston Stump:

> Here lies Bernard Lightfoot who was accidently killed in the forty-fifth year of his age. Erected by his grateful family.

The language we spoke was a broad dialect retaining many syntactical simplicities. In the wolds we had flat, hyphenated vowels and diphthongs that boomed like gongs, as if we were stone deaf. Tennyson, who came from nearby Somersby, illustrated in his ballad 'Northern Farmer, New Style', our distinctive speech:

> But I knaw'd a Qua-aker feller as often 'as towd ma this:
> 'Do-ant thou marry for munny, but go-a wheer munny is!'

In the fens the accent derived its origin from that of the ancient fenlanders, or 'Gyrwie', who spoke, as the name suggests, with a thin, high-pitched whine acquired over the years to carry their voices above the reeds and grasses of the marshlands. My mother's family, the Pouchers, spoke in this way – which was a pleasant contrast to the thunderous tones of my Dunham uncles. My mother's family was equally divided between wold and fen, her mother a Dunham and her father a Poucher. The name of Dunham is derived from the Danish *Dunhólmr*, meaning 'an area of raised land surrounded by water'. These people from the wolds were blond, thick-set, unsmiling, with large feet, ears and mouths. The Pouchers from the fens were dark, long-nosed and spare. 'Poucher' may mean 'poacher' – in which Lincolnshire abounded; more likely it was an indication of their trade – in leather working, as they came from the hamlet of Tanvats deep in the fens. Alternatively, they may have come by their names from *pêcheur*, living as they did in tidal marshes. Whatever the derivation, in my childhood I found them attractive because their menfolk always seemed to be called Tom, which was our name for penis.

Other Lincolnshire names also reflected the countryside and rural occupations. In the wolds were found Woolman, Sheepshanks, Fleecer, Fielder, Clover, Warren, Tupp, Hogg, Hare, Shearer, Chitterling and, of course, Wold. There were few industrial names: no Weavers, Goldsmiths, Knapps, Wrights, Corders or Colliers, but there were, however, Gaunts in plenty. (Presumably this name did not derive from *gant*, implying glovemaker, but Ghent from whence, as did our own John of Gaunt of Old Bolingbroke, they came.) Nevertheless, in the market towns there were plenty of rural trade names – Thatcher, Chandler, Farrier, Wicket, Skinner, Harness and Chapman. Lane from *laine* and Kemp meaning comber spoke

... he continued to wear clogs

of the wool trade. Gault and Grice, local names for a pig, were often found as family names in the more remote villages, as did those ending in bottom: Rainsbottom and Rowbottom. A bottom in Lincolnshire is the river-fed valley lying between the wolds.

Where the wolds gave way to the fens the names changed abruptly and carried with them the description not of occupation so much as that of the enclosed world of the marshes and tidal saltings: Drake, Snape, Snipe, Spratt, Sprott, Pen, Swan, Rook, Thraile, Gosling, Poll and Elver spoke of the fauna. From the land itself came Ford, Syke, Crick, Mudd, Morris, Leach, Myers and Bourne. The oldest wetland trades of all, Fisher, Fuller, Fowler, Ferrier and even Poucher abounded as family names.

The dominating figure in my mother's life (I never knew him, for he died shortly before I was born) was her grandfather Dunham, whose feet were splayed, as the local wags pointed out 'at a quarter to three'. His flat-footedness and heavy gait – which I, alas, have inherited – earned him the nickname of 'Booty' Dunham. He typified the prosperous wold farmer of a

... reputed to have very fine ankles

century ago; independent and stubborn to a degree in that he continued to wear clogs, stuffed with straw after the Dutch fashion, long after he had accumulated a fortune and retired to a more comfortable existence. Plagued by rheumatism in old age, he had rigged up in his house in West Street a rope-operated chair-hoist to heave him upstairs to bed – a nightly task performed in rotation by his grandsons. The richer and older he got, the more marked were his Pecksniffian qualities, shared also by my great-grandmother, Elizabeth Dunham. On the occasion of Jane's birth Muriel was sent round to West Street to convey the good news and was handed a sixpenny bit for the baby and the admonition 'Tha-ats all thou'll git. Go-a tell thy Ma not to 'ave any mo-ah of them little beggars!'

In sharp contrast, though frequently intermarried with the Dunhams, the Pouchers from the fens had none of the blunt, heavy-handedness of their relatives from the wolds. Their menfolk were reputed to have very fine ankles – shown to advantage at the time I was a child by the then-fashion of wearing plus-fours. Certainly they were nimble-footed, as their Gyrwie forebears would have had to be, depending as they did on stilts to pick their way over the marshes. Isolated in their watery land, these Poucher families nevertheless appreciated and perhaps even relished the stark beauty of their surroundings and left records of it in evocative paintings in oil and watercolour. But the daily grind of ploughing, planting and picking, enlivened only by what home-made entertainments they could devise or, on Sundays by the chapel bell tolling across the flat acres, led some to depart the fens to follow the trades of herbalist or apothecary – a far cry from the harsh potato fields and sugar beet plantations of home. I see them as descendants of the shy, strange Gyrwies whom the Romans either enslaved or drove deep into the fens and were called by their conquerors *Iceni*.

When we were young we always referred to anyone whose behaviour was a little strange or outlandish as 'ickeny', with the emphasis, in true Lincolnshire speech, on the second syllable. No one in the immediate family was more 'ickeny' than my wicked Uncle Jack Poucher – as I was subsequently to learn to my advantage.

... carried ~~off,~~ inadvertently, ~~the~~ gilded cock

*U*ncle Jack was Poucher by name but Dunham by temperament. Quite why he was also 'wicked' was never properly established. In the interests of teaching us good behaviour, however, he was ingenious at devising punishments that were both painful and humiliating. We saw them as acts of spite, even though overlain by a veneer of sanctimoniousness. Frank when young was much given to lobbing his elbows on the table during meals. Uncle Jack could not abide this and, finding his admonitions ignored, once inserted drawing pins under the table cloth on either side of Frank's place. Another time, on a Sunday seaside outing when Harold had inadvertently flicked sand into the picnic sandwiches, he promptly seized the boy and suspended him by his braces from a post over the breakwater and left him to dangle in the encroaching tide.

Uncle Jack's wickedness also embraced his being a skinflint. In an 'ickeny' way, his parsimony was thrown into greater relief by his very rare bouts of profligacy. When his cousin, Langton Dunham, was shot by a sniper a few minutes after eleven o'clock on 11 November 1918, my uncle, serving with the Canadian Signals, was up the line visiting the Lincolns. On witnessing his cousin's death, 'He spent,' as my mother put it, 'his very last shilling sending me a telegram so that I would break the news to Langton's parents.' In recounting this incident the emphasis was always placed on the senseless waste, not of poor Langton but of Uncle Jack's last bob.

To rush to bear ill tidings, however, was not uncharacteristic of Uncle Jack, whose presence in these pages is recorded mainly because he epitomized the two branches of the genetic tree that converged in my mother's generation. To give him his full name, John Mellor (named most appropriately after the judge who, finding my great-grandfather guilty of slandering a fellow horse coper, awarded only a farthing in damages) departed England for Canada where he prospered, much to the irritation of those who had bid him good riddance rather than godspeed. He then returned in 1915 with the Canadian Overseas Contingent and survived three years in the trenches, albeit wounded.

Wounded heroes are easy meat for local beauties. Convalescing in Derbyshire, Uncle Jack met and subsequently married such a one. Aunt Rosa Proctor was not only beautiful but elegant, with a great sense of style. Not without her shortcomings, she chattered incessantly and had a wide smile that revealed an uncommon amount of gold in her teeth, when Lincolnshire women of her age might expect to be toothless. She endeared herself to my father, however, because of her green thumb. The cotoneaster she planted and subsequently espaliered against the river warehouse wall did indeed, as my father prophesied, in later years hold up the building, not the reverse. It was his soft spot for her that prompted him to declare that she came from Congleton or Matlock Bath, or wherever, anywhere in fact than from the fair village of Bakewell. For that would not do. As head of a business house that included a confectionery, he had no wish to see his brother-in-law's bride come to be known as the Bakewell Tart. He profited from the sale of many thousands of them each year. Similar to the *tarte Alsacienne*, the Bakewell tart had a thin, pastry case layered with jam and filled with a mixture of almonds, breadcrumbs and ground rice. Kept for a week, a Bakewell tart was at its best particularly when eaten with a good thick slice of Cheshire or Wensleydale cheese. For me, though, Aunt Rosa's virtue lay in her scolding my tortoises when they went off on their inexplicable wanderings across the Market Place.

Our granary cats were semi-wild. Dogs came and went. No animal, domestic or otherwise, was ever allowed indoors so they seldom laid claim to our affections. The tortoises, however, were not only the denizens of the garden, they were also the companions of my childhood. In spite of their unique status, they were nameless because they were – to my eyes – indistinguishable and I felt they should each bear the same name; but I balked at choosing one.

The anomaly was resolved by a colonial cousin, Harry, son of Aunt Florence, the aunt whose sartorial shortcomings my father viewed with such misgiving. Every five years Harry would return on furlough from East Africa and spend part of his leave with us. He was fond of my father, after whom he was named, and of Lincolnshire, for he had trained during the First World War at nearby Cranwell in what was then the Royal Flying Corps and was reputed to have carried off, inadvertently, the gilded cock of the weathervane atop Lincoln Cathedral while on a training flight in a Sopwith Camel.

In insisting that the tortoises be named, Harry bore in mind my requirement. In a little ceremony in our summerhouse he dubbed them 'Poley' and 'Poley', explaining to my satisfaction that 'polé-polé' in Kiswahili meant 'slowly'. Aunt Rosa was present on this occasion, and she mentioned to me that the strange promptings that drove my tortoises on their periodic excursions across the Market Place were little different from those that made us all clamour every weekend to be taken to the seaside.

This remark had a more profound effect on me than perhaps was intended. The notion that humans had retained certain animal characteristics quickened my growing interest in biological pursuits. Moreover, it led me to reject the obverse, that animals had human qualities inherent in them. This, with a certain amount of relief on my part, released me from practically all of my childhood storybooks, marinated as most of them were in anthropomorphism, leaving my mind fallow for what was to follow.

Perhaps it was time to emerge from the cocoon of early childhood, which in my case took the form of 'the Maud', a constant source of comfort and protection. The Maud was an old plaid horse blanket about a yard of which had been folded back from one end and the sides stitched up. Thus on any outing in the car when the weather was cold or wet, it was wonderful to slide my legs into the sack part so that the stitched flap came up under my backside, and to pull the rest round my shoulders to enter a warm, cosy world of thick, coarse wool, albeit with a strong, feral smell. I never knew why it was called 'the Maud', but it may have been a local corruption of the word 'maund' meaning a basket.

As a family we did not need to go beyond the confines of our relatives and employees or even outside the immediate family for company. But the difference between me and my much older brothers and sisters was that I became convinced of the need for wider horizons. We lived in a rural setting in a small market town that could be characterized as being socially and religiously intolerant. Within this island we ourselves practised our own personal brand of nonconformity. As the early Quakers found, having left England and the Low Countries to seek religious freedom in New England, they were soon persecuted by the majority of the Puritans, who had not sailed to the New World to permit anything of the sort, but to indulge in their own special brand of intolerance.

Our isolation was self-imposed. It took strange forms, of which I can remember two. We mispronounced the names of people for whom we did not care, or with whom we did not feel comfortable. Great-aunt Rachel Poucher's maid, Fleecer, was really called Felicia (she came from a small group of families of Spanish origin brought over by Catherine of Aragon as part of her household). We respected but did not love Great-uncle Alfred Dunham's servant, Mackinder, who wore a wig. When he was about some household chore he would remove his wig, roll it up in a newspaper and put a duster on his head. When he died it transpired that his name was not Mackinder, but McAdoo and he was the last surviving member of the family of Mrs Woodrow Wilson.

This habit of mangling names may have owed as much to our carelessness with language, which was the object of continual parental admonition, as to a kind of defence against those outside our own very private circle. No such excuse can be found for the elaborate practical jokes that were played on outsiders, almost as if they were rites of passage. They were designed not so much to amuse the joker as to humiliate the victim. They usually involved water and conveyed the unmistakable implication that those who fell for them demonstrated thereby some moral shortcoming. The two most popular with us were the funnel trick and the umbrella stand-off.

We would lure the victim, usually in his Sunday finery, into the yard where my brothers would demonstrate the money-making trick. Frank would stick a funnel in the top of Harold's

... the funnel trick

trousers and place a three-penny bit on his forehead. After a lot of oohs and aahs, Harold would bob his head down and, if the coin fell into the funnel, he was allowed to pocket it. The visitor would clamour for a chance at such easy money and his greed would cause him to throw caution to the winds. The contestant would tilt his head back so that Harold could place the anticipated prize on his forehead. This my brother would appear to do by licking the silver coin and pressing it firmly on to the victim's brow, then deftly removing and pocketing it. The butt of the joke, with the funnel securely in place, gazing skywards and jaw hanging slackly, would put out his arm to steady his aim. At this moment, Muriel would dart out from behind him and empty a jug of water down the funnel. The interval, while the cold water found its way down the funnel to the victim's genitals, was always one for paralytic mirth.

If a visitor were drawing excessive attention to herself, for instance, she would be invited to assist in the umbrella stand-off. Harold would stand on a kitchen chair holding a glass of water in one hand and an umbrella in the other (preferably the one kept in the scullery which had the fabric rotted and torn). He would place a glass of water against the ceiling and very carefully push the ferrule of the umbrella firmly against the base of the glass. Then he would ask his unsuspecting assistant to hold the handle of the umbrella and press it hard while he stepped down from the chair. This he would place just out of reach and we would all leave the kitchen, abandoning the hapless victim either to a long wait before being rescued, or a wetting. The more enterprising would use the umbrella for the purpose for which it was invented, only to find on opening it that the cover was full of holes.

The taking of brass rubbings was in those days an unusual pastime, but much indulged in by Harold on wet afternoons in the school holidays. As with most of his undertakings it had its conspiratorial side. I would be dispatched to beg a ball of cobbler's wax from Hogg, while Harold half-inched a roll or two of rice paper from under the head baker's nose. He took plenty, for he had a habit of munching it absentmindedly as we went along. To Scrivelsby we would go, where there was a small brass effigy of an early Dymoke, or to Tattershall for a headless Cromwell, and sometimes to Ashby Puerorum where, after taking our brass rubbing we could scrump apples from Uncle Tommy Dunham's orchard.

Once in the church we would unroll the rice paper over the brass and anchor each corner with a hymn book, and then set to work with the ball of wax. At Scrivelsby, however, the best results were to be obtained if Harold could cajole the sexton into taking off his boots and treading down the rice paper in his stockinged feet. The best day for this was a Friday or a Saturday when the sexton's thick, woollen socks, after a week's use, imparted to the rice paper just the right texture to produce a sharp, clear imprint.

In summer our self-imposed isolation was delectable. Long days in the canoe, or Sunday trips to the sea while other children crept unwillingly to Sunday school were satisfying enough. But for much of the year the differences were less enjoyable. We took the *News Chronicle*, a liberal daily owned by the Quaker Cadburys. Consequently, I joined the junior readers' club and wore a beautifully enamelled badge with a bear on it and learned the members' secret recognition signal. Sadly, there was no one with whom to exchange passwords, for the parents of my schoolmates read high Tory journals such as the *Daily Mail* and the *Daily Express* and sported badges with Teddy Tail or Rupert. Owned as these papers were by jingoistic press barons, I could look upon their youthful adherents with disdain. But righteousness was not enough, and gradually I came to realize that it was no good not being part of the Great Game of Life.

Every spring, too, brought its forcible reminder that isolation, however splendid, was purchased at a price. Quite simply, we never knew what was going on before it actually happened. It did not matter so much that I missed whatever mysterious signal announced to the children of the town that hoops should be raced in the streets, or the day when spinning tops were in fashion. Frank and Harold had tall, spindly tops known as 'window-breakers'. They would hurtle through the air at the crack of a whip to land across the yard where they would innocently resume their spinning. These tops had an air of recklessness about them that I found irresistible. My sister Jane, intercepting the gleam in my eye, hastily produced for me the squat, stumpy top that proceeded at a slow, Lincoln-shire mudbound gait regardless of how hard I flogged it. But no harm was done if I greeted the morning hoop-less or top-less, for the omission could easily be repaired at lunchtime.

Oak Apple Day, however, was something very different. The twenty-ninth of May was the anniversary of King Charles II's Restoration in 1660 – he having eight years earlier escaped his pursuers after the battle of Worcester by hiding in the branches of an oak tree. So, on May the twenty-ninth we wore oak leaves or silvered acorns or 'oak apples' in our caps, and woe betide any lad who appeared in the school yard without a favour in his cap or lapel. He would immediately be faced with the prospect of having to run the gauntlet between two lines of jeering schoolmates brandishing bunches of stinging nettles. It always seemed to me, all unbeknowing as I set out for school, Oak Apple Day had to be the one day in the year that my stockings were garterless and my trousers hitched up higher than usual – and this before the day when Kathleen had revealed to me the soothing properties of dock leaves on nettle stings.

I realized, too, that it was not enough to be an observer: one had to be a participant. In a negative way I sensed that I was not cast for the role of the former. Observers kept diaries. When I tried this, the entries faded by the second day. The prince opened vistas, but they were always over the rim of the horizon. Also, he himself, while providing vicarious experience, was inexorably drawn into the family rather than drawing it out. So, I made my first reconnaissance of the outside world. Why not, through my mother's Methodist connexion, join the Boys' Brigade? Its aims were, however, somewhat restricted:

> The advancement of Christ's Kingdom among Boys, and the promotion of habits of Obedience, Reverence, Discipline and Self-Respect and all that tends towards true Christian Manliness.

I adjusted my protective layer of Thermogene and inspected closer. The Brigade wore blue serge suits, polished boots (I had neither) and wore a bandolier and a pillbox hat like sepoys in the Indian Mutiny. To the blare of bugles and the rattle of drums they marched to chapel on a Sunday evening. They exercised with rifles from which the action bolts had been removed.

All this suggested obstacles. But what put the lid on ambition in this quarter was the jingle that went to their marching tune:

> We are the Boys' Brigade
> Covered in Marmalade,
> A tuppeny ha'penny pillbox
> And half a yard of braid.

I was a notoriously messy eater particularly where breakfast marmalade was concerned. Without regret I dismissed the matter of joining the Brigade, for I had other fish to fry. A troop of Boy Scouts had been formed under the scout mastership of the gallant young rector of Thimbleby.

My father, in an attempt to improve not only my writing but also the ordering of my thoughts, which were pursued like rabbits in the harvest field, had suggested I read the newspaper leading articles. This I did, in a desultory way and only intermittently, greatly preferring the Duke of Wellington's dispatches, to which I had been introduced by the prince. The Iron Duke's tactics I also studied to more immediate effect. First, learn the terrain: to do this I acquired through a Poucher cousin a dog-eared edition of *Scouting for Boys*. This book became my most treasured possession. The next step was to reconnoitre. The Thimbleby troop met too far away for this, but I found a substitute in the Brownies, who foregathered in a disused schoolroom under the leadership of a formidable lady Brown Owl. Blessed with long sight, I perched in a window

... A tuppeny ha'penny pillbox and half a yard of braid

embrasure and followed the knot-tying lessons with a lace pulled from one of my boots. Eventually, of course, I was found out and had to retreat. It was, I decided, time to confront my father with my ambition.

The three grounds on which the refusal was kindly but firmly based were that he had no wish to see me parading about in uniform with a bunch of yahoos; I was too young; and, unless I had been baptized in the Church of England (as it was a church troop), admission was impossible.

Wars are seldom fought without allies, however, and these I found in the prince and Uncle Jack, who was with us on a prolonged stay while recovering from some illness or other. I discussed with them the grounds for my father's refusal and sent them off on my behalf to establish a bridgehead.

Behind the back staircase was a short tunnel at cellar level which led from the larder to a small cubby that passed as an office for my father on quarter days when rents were due. I heard the prince go down the steps into the cubby with my father one evening and wriggled along the tunnel and un-latched the cellar door so that I could hear what was being discussed. The prince argued a good case: 'Come, Francis, while I recognize that Boy is too young, there is no cub pack for him to join and it is only fair that he should be accommodated in the troop somehow or other. In India we made them water carriers, remember?' This was not too wise a parallel, and cut no ice with my father. The prince, always ready to switch, in true Russian fashion, when encountering stiff resistance, moved to other ground.

'Have you thought, Francis, how the first and last of your reservations really cancel one another out? I gather that the only marching the troop does is about four times a year to church, and surely Boy would not be expected to parade on such occasions?' And so it was left for my father to mull over. But a breach had definitely been made. Now for the assault.

It was at this point that wicked Uncle Jack took over. He pointed out to me that I could not pretend to be older than I was, so I had to show that my age did not matter. This could best be done by concentrating on one thing. He decided to teach me morse code and, to throw in for good measure, how to semaphore, as it was just as easy to learn both at the same time. File cards were marked up with morse and semaphore. A long roll of wrapping paper was pinned on the ceiling above my bed with opposites (A opposite N, B opposite V and so on) all lined up. Within a few days I thought I was proficient enough to be tested. The prince sprawled in his wicker chair in the garden with Uncle Jack perched on a kitchen stool, both dispelling the evening cloud of midges with great puffs of cheroot smoke. I, in the rockery above the water steps, took and received my uncle's messages and frantically answered with the flags. As evening drew on out came the flashlights and we changed to morse.

With this impressive skill at my fingertips – a means of communication that far excelled the whistle signals of my brothers – the prince and Uncle Jack led me on Scout Night through the standing barley to Thimbleby. Spotting the troop forming up in the park behind the Rectory, I was hoisted up on a gate and unwrapped my signal flags. My communication over the intervening hundred yards or so was to the effect that I desired admission to the troop. I was, I should say, dressed in an assortment of scouting gear that had laboriously been collected for me by Frank and Harold from junk barrows in the Market. After repeating the message, and after Uncle Jack, peering at the scoutmaster through his binoculars, had assured himself of its reception, we withdrew.

Two weeks of strained silence followed. Then one day, laid out on my bed was an entire scout's uniform. It cost seventeen shillings and ninepence. With Kathleen's help, who deftly jettisoned my Thermogene – for it had been a wet summer – I clambered into my gear. I cannot remember whether anyone accompanied me to Scout Night, but I must have danced over the hill.

On arrival I saluted the scout master and then tripped over my signal flags and dropped *Scouting for Boys*. Re-assembled with the help of several pairs of rough hands, I was chided for wanting to join a troop to which I could never belong. However, under the circumstances (which were not divulged),

I was told I could remain but not be a member of a patrol. I would have to stand on parade alone at the bottom of the square formed by the other three patrols. My feelings were of indescribable joy.

Reinforcements were needed, however, if I was not to remain a barely tolerated outsider. At school I found a quiet, white-haired boy called Pratt to whom I taught morse very quickly. I then recruited a fiery red-head called Carrots O'Connor. (I was forbidden to play with him because his parents were Roman Catholic and his father *drank*.) Finally I found a new arrival, an olive-skinned smiling boy called Sirdar Smith, whose father had died of wounds in Waziristan in 1927. This motley crew I presented to the scout master, not on Scout Night but, as suggested by the prince, privately.

Further consultations must have taken place. Weekly subventions to the scout fund were apparently guaranteed by my father. My private army presented itself in a motley of bits of uniform, for I had shared mine out. We were told of the restrictions that were to apply. We could form ourselves as a patrol but could never be full members of the troop. We would henceforth be known as the Foreign Legion and would always be at the bottom of the pecking order. We would never be permitted to parade.

Consequently, we could not trek with the troop to the annual scout camp among the fallow deer in the park at Scrivelsby, home of the Dymoke family, hereditary champions of England since the fourteenth century. Instead we were driven there in great style, although my mother refused to allow Carrots in the car because of his religious affiliations. We emptied the capacious box-like boot and envied him his perch behind us in the bottom of it with the lid propped open, tapping all the way on the intervening coach wall, 'A quick brown fox jumps over the lazy dog' to the irritation of the grown-ups and to the delight of the other 'Ickenies' who made up the Foreign Legion.

... reassembled with the help of several pairs of rough hands

FOUR

The Old Rasputin Restoration Society

... handed over two shining steel cans

S t George's Day, the twenty-third of April, brought with it the promise of summer. For on that day the carrier's cart stopped outside and the railway delivery man handed over two shining steel cans emblazoned with the label 'Superior Yacht Varnish 7s. 9d. carriage paid.' It mattered not that St George's Day was when the first cuckoo was heard, or that it was Shakespeare's birthday (as well as the day he died) or that the wind was still strong and was snapping the flag atop the church tower. Who cared? The yacht varnish had arrived.

The red cross on the white ground to commemorate the dubious sanctity of England's patron saint not only flew from but graced the church tower, for it was the one day each year that the eye was diverted from the out-of-proportion 'snuffer' spire that some embellisher had added. But April was still a long way off from real summer, and warm though it might sometimes be, in Lincolnshire we were diligent in following Chaucer's counsel:

> Till May is out, ne'er cast a clout.
> After great heat cometh colde;
> No man caste his pilch away.

My 'pilch' was the wad of Thermogene, which remained thick on my chest until June showed some promise of flaming.

Every year with unfailing regularity on the first day of June, Frank and Harold would place two trestles on the lawn and then invade my private preserve in the bottom warehouse. With a pair of step ladders they would unlash and then lower gingerly the great canoe which, all winter long had been suspended from the warehouse beams above my head, its paddles, back and floor boards stacked on shelves beyond my reach.

My excitement could barely be contained. With characteristic care, Frank washed the canoe inside and out, inspected it and then sanded it down. Eventually satisfied that all was well, coats of the superior yacht varnish were applied. The floor boards and paddles received the same treatment. In an agony of waiting I watched successive layers of varnish being left to harden. Finally a high gloss finish was applied. The boat would then be inverted and the iron shoe that ran from stem to stern tightened and enamelled black. Harold would inspect and paint the stanchions and mooring rings at the foot of the water steps, and attach a new painter. The cushions would be examined with a critical eye by Jane or Muriel and, if necessary, re-covered.

By late June the canoe would be lowered into the water. Even then, the wait did not end for it had to be flooded to the gunwales and left to swell for twenty-four hours. Emptied and dried, floorboards fitted, back boards and cushions put in place, Frank would climb in and take off on his proving cruise. Perched in the stern with the prow high out of the water, Frank drove the canoe at great speed, with the river churning in the wake of the short stern paddle. Even with double paddles I never came near to the velocity with which Frank shot through the water. On his return we always had our treat. Standing on his head, his hands gripping the thwarts amidships, Frank would walk upside down with his feet pressed up to the underside of our bridge and thus pass through to tie up with our new painter. With that display his interest in the canoe lapsed until it was time to move it back to winter quarters.

My father, early in the century, had bought this elegant, roomy, clinker-built canoe. It had been made in Canada for fishing expeditions, but its long, sweeping strakes gave it the look of a Viking long-ship. Seating four comfortably, there was also plenty of room for camp equipment and fishing tackle. It was in this vessel, the most beautiful of our possessions, that Muriel and Kathleen inadvertently sent me arse-over-tip to emulate Ophelia under my straw hat. Many years before I could swim a stroke the canoe became my refuge, my solace and above all my ship that carried me to distant times and far-off lands of the imagination.

Up early on summer mornings, I would take my breakfast with me, so that I could glide by a pair of kingfishers sparkling over the water, flashing their metallic blue wings. If the rooks stopped cawing for a moment I could usually hear a cuckoo. If there was time before school to paddle further to the meadows I could hear the sky full of peewits and larks. In the evenings I would go up river to the water mill and watch the trout rise to hatches of flies, or work my way through the reeds of the overflow dyke that looped around the mill. There I would startle moorhens and bring the bewhiskered water rat out of his bank to see who was disturbing his private demesne.

At night I would lie in bed longing for the morning to come, listening to the sound of the water rippling over the pebbles and the slap-flap of the moorhen's wings as she sought to divert a predator from her nest. Then the swallows, house martins and swifts would return and swoop tirelessly over the water. Trout would rise and fat, sleek chubb and dace lie snug in the dark shadows under the bridge. Even more than walking matches, coarse fishing was a summer recreation in Lincoln-shire. But with dough balls and bacon rind a-dangling from hooks of young hopefuls, I never saw a fish taken from our bridge. No one ever bothered to change his bait, but then,

... feet pressed up to the underside of our bridge

innovation has never been a particularly strong Lincolnshire trait. In British Columbia, in the Jasper Range, I have seen many a brown trout taken from the lake of an evening by a boy who, when the fish would not rise to a fly, baited his hook with miniature marshmallows. In Lincolnshire, even if we had thought of this, we would not have wasted marshmallows on fish.

Below the bridge the Bain broadened out as it flowed past my family's wool warehouses, granaries and coal yards, and ran softly out of the immediate confines of the town. On either side of the river were water meadows and small orchards from which apples were regularly scrumped. A little further on, a stand of massive copper beeches bowed low into the water across the width of the river. Into this green tunnel I would pass, resting my paddle while I looked, with carefully controlled sentiment, at the dank, weed-covered river steps from which a beautiful young girl had slipped to her death. Had she not become the spirit of the place, like Sabrina drifting down the Severn? Gliding under the great trees I used to feel her presence: happily not a sombre but a cheerful, almost impish ghost.

Emerging, the river opened up under a dilapidated cow bridge to what was rather grandly known as 'Three Rivers'. It was really the junction of the Bain with its tributary the Waring, and the canal. A staunch, or weir, had made the Bain unnavigable without making a portage, and the canal was dense with weeds, in the shadow of which many brave boys were known to have tickled pike. At this point the Bain and the canal alongside it began their journey to join the Witham at Dogdyke, recalling Tennyson's brook:

> With many a curve my banks I fret
> By many a field and fallow.
> And many a fairy foreland set
> With willow-weed and mallow.

The canoe became the headquarters of the Old Rasputin Restoration Society. The prince was only too willing to share my enthusiasm for the history of our locality, but he did so in certain terms that required each incident to be examined with a fresh mind and eye, disregarding what historians had to tell us – for he thought them prisoners of prevailing passions and prejudices. To this I agreed, after my experience with the sycamore. My father had planted sycamores where my mother had wanted a copper beech. He refused, as he said, incorrectly, that it would spoil the lawn and, correctly, that its roots growing towards the river would undermine the wall from which tumbled in summer a great curtain of rambler roses. Perceiving the sycamore to be a dull tree, and a harbourer of midges of an evening, I could not bring myself to believe that Zaccheus, however short in stature, would have climbed into its branches to see Jesus pass by. Our researches revealed, however, that that tree was not our plane variety but a kind of oriental fig.

Things are not what they seem. Nor, said the prince, are people. He had in mind some lurid article in a 'penny dreadful', as my father called the popular tabloids, on the life and loves of the monk Rasputin. In spite of being an evil-smelling fellow with rather gruesome personal habits, Rasputin had assumed a dominant position in the court at St Petersburg. The prince pointed out that Rasputin, villified as he was, not only saved the Tsarevitch's life on more than one occasion, but in the heady days of July and August 1914 alone warned against going to war, and pitting Russian troops against the combined might of Austria–Hungary and Germany. So we decided that our researches should be undertaken in a spirit of enquiry that might restore the monk's reputation as one who had a good sense of the true relation and proportion of events. We thus incorporated ourselves as the Rasputin Restoration Society. I wished to add 'Royal', as in the Royal And Ancient Order of Buffaloes, to which for some mysterious reason my brother Harold belonged. This would not do, said the prince, as Rasputin was not of royal blood. But the title still looked bald and lacking in dignity, so we added 'Old' to give the Society a touch of verisimilitude.

I recruited into the Society my red-haired friend who had

61

... who could staunch haemorrhage by hypnosis

joined me in the Foreign Legion. He came because he wanted to ride in the canoe and show us how to tickle pike. My mother could not be approached, although she had a lively sense of history, for she would have known that Rasputin was a monk and therefore an object of her Methodist hostility. My father was reluctant but eventually overcame his reservations as he had a soft spot for the Tsarevitch. Not that my father was a royalist – if anything he was a republican. But he often referred to himself – much to the amusement of local wags – as being 'a great bleeder', and anyone who could staunch haemorrhage by hypnosis was worthy of remembrance.

Our first expedition with the Society was to the strange and haunted corner of the three rivers, the site of a Roman maze. We never did find out what part a maze played in Roman rites or ceremonies. It was a melancholy place, but not a bad one at which to start our search for the original Roman settlement, for when the Romans first came to Horncastle the Gyrwie, the fen dwellers – who were just shuffling out of the Iron Age – were enslaved by their new masters to dig the canal and the drainage systems. From Cambridgeshire, the original home of the Iceni, they dug Car Dyke, some seventy miles of water-way, to link up with our Witham. The prince suggested that they settled on the banks of the river to grow food and fodder for the legions and their cavalry. The soils were rich and, when well drained, highly productive, and as we found was still the case, the salt winds from the North Sea kept crops relatively free from fly infestation and disease. We also noticed, when exploring up river, that our water steps represented the highest point of navigation. Above, there were no more rings or stanchions, but becks, fords and mills. North along the broad bottom of the Bain the river became a stream and eventually a brook when it reached the Dunham water mill. Below our bridge were the wharves from which the family barges plied, carrying corn and the wool clip and returning with seed potatoes, coal and agricultural implements.

Once the summer holidays began the prince was my regular companion in the canoe. He learned, like an old campaigner, to make himself comfortable. Refusing to wear plimsolls in the boat, he met my stringent requirements in such matters by donning over his boots a discarded pair of Harold's football stockings. In the capacious poacher's pocket in his Norfolk jacket the prince kept a tin box of his favourite Havanas and a silver tankard in a soft leather bag. A bottle of 'cough medicine' was trailed on hot days in the water at the end of a piece of string.

In our Quaker household, built on a rigid substratum of Methodism, such high standards of personal rectitude and self-discipline were expected that life would have been intolerable without more than the usual dose of English hypocrisy. The bottle of Jamaica rum – to which was added a touch of rhubarb juice when the prince was costive – was known as 'cough medicine'. For if it were not, how could he consume it in an otherwise strictly tee-total family? I remained in ignorance of the real nature of this elixir, although I did occasionally wonder why Belton replenished the bottle not at the chemist but at the dram shop in the Saracen's Head.

Hypocrisy mixed with hefty amounts of prejudice made for domestic harmony, and we lived on mighty dollops of both. They applied not only to strong drink. My sister Jane, though not overtly pious, was without doubt my self-appointed moral guardian. Told off by her for defiantly sticking my thumb up my nose and not only extending but *twiddling* my fingers at her – in response to being chastised for something (like being late for tea) – she flushed angrily and told me in icy tones that such a disgusting gesture was 'WORSE THAN SWEARING'. Furthermore, she said I 'must have learned that from that Carrots O'Connor'. This did not surprise me, for we lived in a closed-in world, but could there be anything 'worse than swearing'?

None of us swore. The prince out of deference to my family only occasionally swore in Turkish, which of course no one understood except Uncle Morton. But we found our expletives in a rudimentary rhyming slang: 'By Goy! You son of a stitch! You boggering, ruddy, muddy bucket of pitch!' The father of one of Jane's admirers, a Methodist lay-preacher, was so inventive in invective that he was known throughout his life as 'Bloomin'' Chapman.

When it came to gambling we were not interested, except when a Poucher great-aunt invited us to tea. Having made short work of her plum bread and chocolate cake out would come the green baize and the ivory chips. Sometimes ex-soldier uncles gathered and we would play *vingt-et-un* with them for matches. This was never allowed at home. One rainy day, though, Muriel, Harold and I, feeling bored, crept up to the attic to play – with coppers for we could not find any spare matches. Piles of pennies, halfpennies and farthings were soon changing hands. Overtaken by gambling fever we did not notice Jane's sedate and dedicated prowl, adopted by her when she detected a whiff of moral turpitude. Suddenly she swooped and swept away our game, leaving us chastened with our overturned table rather like the money-changers in the temple. Peace was only restored when my mother was called to sit in judgement. 'After all,' she said, with the little smile she reserved for such occasions, 'they were only using coins as if they were matches!'

A bottle of "cough medicine" was trailed on hot days in the water

Hypocrisy slept peacefully in the arms of prejudice. It oozed around our lives like treacle impregnating suet pudding. Of course, superstition and pagan rites were eschewed. For instance, the Quaker week began with First Day, not Sunday. We confidently walked under ladders and never 'touched wood' or threw spilt salt over our shoulders. Such lapses into paganism might have been passed over, but any suggestion of popery caused swift reaction. Saints were virtually a closed book. In any case I thought they were dull fellows – with one exception. He was St Lawrence, Horncastle's patron saint, whose emblem was painted on a great drum clock above the butcher's shop in the High Street. He was one of five deacons martyred in Rome by the Emperor Valerian in AD 258 by being roasted on a gridiron. His last words were reputed to be: '*Assum est; versa et manduca!*' ('I am well done; turn me over and eat me!'). Few knew of this, which was a pity for it would have appealed to the sardonic humour of the townspeople who never ate meat that was not thoroughly charred! St Lawrence's gridiron was painted in gold leaf on the black, curving side of the drum, which was mounted on an elaborate bracket set high above the pavement and which contained on either face the ornate gilded hands and figures of the clock. One Christmas Muriel decided to disregard the Quaker practice of not celebrating Christian festivals and make a Christmas cake. This she duly did, and on top of the icing reproduced a convincing version of Lawrence's gridiron. Belton, on being asked to admire it, enquired about the significance of the decoration. On being told, 'By Goy!' he said, 'I allus' thought it were a muck fork!'

When the Society reconvened in the following year I flashed this new piece of knowledge to the prince with a wave of the arm as we passed under the clock. The prince, while seemingly impressed, suggested that scraps of information were no substitute for real erudition. In keeping with the principles of the Society why not cast aside bigotry in a search for home-grown saints? And where better to look than at the sites of Lincolnshire's two great monastic foundations, Bardney and Partney?

We had to wait for a Wednesday afternoon – early closing day – when Frank could be prevailed upon to drive us to Partney. We always rattled through Partney on our summer trips to the seaside at Skegness, but we had never stopped to explore this small, pretty village, the last on the wolds before the road dropped down to the fenlands at Burgh-le-Marsh. On this occasion, our one and only visit as it happened, we drew a blank as far as monastic remains were concerned, so turned and headed back for Bardney, some twenty miles the other side of Horncastle. Here, where the Witham was crossed by a narrow, drovers' bridge, we found the village in its setting of root crops and potato fields, dominated then as now by no more splendid monument to civilization than a gigantic sugar beet refinery. No trace of an ancient abbey, except for a single clue in the church – a stone slab bearing the effigy of perhaps the last abbot, Richard Horncastle, before the monastery was destroyed in the sixteenth century.

It was while looking for something in my father's library quite unconnected with our present researches that the prince, idly thumbing through a copy of Bede, made the rewarding discovery that Bardney had, in fact, once housed the remains of both a saint and a king. The king was Oswald, a seventh-century ruler in Northumbria, a Christian, a bit of a tyrant, but one who during his short reign had acquired some saintly attributes along the way – giving alms to the poor and praying for the souls of his fallen soldiers. We took the book to the attic, away from prying eyes, and the prince regaled me with the story of Oswald's death at the hands of the King of Mercia, who cut off the dead king's head and limbs and impaled them for public viewing. The date was August the fifth in the year 642. The following year Oswald's brother, Oswy, who had succeeded him as King of Northumbria, slew the King of Mercia and married his own daughter, Osthrida, to Ethelred, the new king. Osthrida and Ethelred were much attached to the monastery at Bardney and decided to bury her uncle's bones in the Abbey church. But when Osthrida came with the cortège she found the gates barred against her and the monks prepared to offer armed resistance; as Mercians they had no wish to entertain the bones of an enemy king. The queen retreated to the banks of the Witham and made camp, her relative's relics placed for safe keeping in a tent. That night a column of incandescent light rose from the canopy and ascended to the heavens. The great light shone until dawn, a marvel that could be seen throughout Lindsey. The next day the monks, after a hasty meeting and not wanting to look a gift horse in the mouth, threw open the gates of Bardney to welcome the queen and her procession. From then on not only did St Oswald's remains heal the sick of the flux and epilepsy, but the soil into which the water drained after it had been used to wash the saint's bones was found to have miraculous, curative properties. Even the abbess of Partney came to beg some of the sacred soil.

One August the fifth, as it happened, my mother was with us as we were coming back from an expedition to Walesby. We paused on Scamblesby Top and looked across the Witham bottom towards Bardney. In the setting sun we were suddenly dazzled by a great shaft of light shining from the site of the former monastery. The members of the Society were struck in wonderment. Not so my mother: 'Look!' she cried, with a hint of mischief in her voice, 'look how the new roof on the Bardney sugar beet factory reflects the sunlight!' The spell was broken.

These discoveries took place when the Society was in its heyday, possibly in 1932. It did not actually decline in the years that followed, but it was overtaken by other interests. In fact, the last expedition was mounted about 1934 as a result of the prince finding a common link in the history of his country and mine. We were up in the attic tracing the outlines of the windows that had been bricked up to avoid the eighteenth-century window tax, and which no one had bothered to open up after the tax had been repealed. My mother always called this disused room 'the Ark'. Perhaps she meant 'arc' for arctic, for it was always cold at that end of the house. I explained to the prince that this was what we called the 'new' part, and we leant out of the mansard window to see the date 1620 carved in the brick at the time it was built. This find rekindled the prince's interest in our Society.

'Boy!' he exclaimed, '1620 was about the beginning of the "troubled times" in Russia when Dmitry was Tsar.' Dmitry was the ruler whose bizarre end was mentioned more than once by way of admonition when I had been careless or reckless in disregarding my elders. 'It was one thing to take baths, but refusing to cross himself in the approved manner was simply asking for trouble, and then letting it be known he took naps in the afternoon was considered the giddy limit. So the Boyars killed him and shot his ashes westward out of a cannon.'

'Sounds to me as if he were a bit "ickeny",' I observed. But the point of the lesson was noted even if it was never taken entirely to heart.

When I told my mother of the 'troubled times' in Russia she reminded me of our own turbulent period in the Civil War, and how the first cavalry engagement had been fought in 1643 on the edge of what was now her land. She had inherited a farm on the wolds out at Hameringham and suggested we accompany her on her next visit. My father had just bought, to the delight of us all, a large black car which we called the George-Marina. It had been made especially for the newly-married Duke and Duchess of Kent, but they did not care for it, perhaps because it had rear side windows which limited their privacy.

With Brown at the wheel we set off for the battle site at Winceby, calling first at Horncastle's parish church to view the hatchment to Sir Ingram Hopton, who was killed in that very skirmish 'in the attempt of seizing the Arch-rebel'. We then moved on to look at the iron ring inserted in one of the pillars in the nave, where tradition has it that the 'Arch-rebel', Cromwell, had tethered his charger on the eve of the fight. But the prince liked the screed that recounted something of the ebb and flow of history. The rector of Horncastle at the time, one Gibson, a fervent royalist, was constantly being imprisoned by Cromwell, but in 1660 recovered his living on the restoration of Charles the Second. The prince read out: 'He lived in such times when Truth to the CHURCH and Loyalty to the KING met with Punishment due only to the worst of crimes.' The screed goes on to record his triumphant return:

. . . at the Head of Several hundred of his Friends.
As his enemies never forgave his Zeal to the Church and
Crown so nothing but the height of Christian Charity
could
Forgive the insults he met from them.

But in 1643 Cromwell had driven out the royalist Mr Gibson,
spent the night in Horncastle and the next had ridden out to
join his troops coming up from Kings Lynn. They were intent
on maintaining the siege of Old Bolingbroke Castle, where the
holed-up royalists had refused to surrender. A royal relief
force was on its way, but Cromwell intercepted them at
Winceby. It was only a skirmish and had no strategic value; its
importance lay in Cromwell showing that his newly trained
cavalry was as good as the king's – if not better.

We followed the road that Cromwell had taken from Horncastle over the Dunham Hills to Winceby. In the car, with a
large-scale map on which were placed all my mounted lead
soldiers, the Society sat and listened as my mother pointed to the
dip in the land below us: 'Slash Hollow it was called afterwards,
for there the parliamentarians caught the cavaliers and put them
to the sword.' She put her right hand across her breast in a very
characteristic gesture. 'Knee deep in blood it was, for they were
trapped in the blackthorn thickets and had no escape,' and made a
little gasp as she caught her breath for dramatic effect.

Later, up in front of the car with Brown on the way home, I
must have fallen asleep dreaming of armies clashing by night. I
heard the stamp and neigh of steeds, the shouts and strange
oaths of their riders and the clink of bridles. I awoke with a
start as we nosed our way round the Bull Ring before turning
into our own street. The summer evening was rich with the
stench of men and horses and the smell of leather. The streets
were jammed with cavalry mounts, hunters, dray and van
horses, great Clydesdales and creamy Suffolk Punches, ponies
and shire horses. Every breed and condition of horseflesh was
there being cajoled, wheedled and threatened by a hundred
grooms, ostlers and dark-faced gypsies. It was the eve of The
Great August Horse Fair.

... dreaming of armies clashing by night

FIVE

Nunkie's Dragon

... *watched with mounting horror*

*I*n 1923, the year I was born, our new maid, Burton, took up residence. She was gloomy and melancholic – which is not surprising as she hailed from Walesby, a bleak village in the northern wolds where her namesake, Robert Burton, who had been rector there in the seventeenth century, wrote *The Anatomy of Melancholy*. I was her special charge but have little recollection of her except that she wore shoes always too large for her feet, and this gave her a step that was unmistakable – like the clippety-clop-clop of the pony that drew the governess cart being led down the yard. Chiefly, though, Burton was remembered in the family for her sad countenance and general woebegone air; but then Lincolnshire had more than its fair share of melancholics, a condition afflicting wold and fen dweller alike. A later cleric at dismal Walesby, Thomas Malthus, perhaps received his inspiration for his great work on population from the sad history of his former living. The village was very nearly wiped out in the Black Death and remained, for centuries after, a forlorn and forgotten place. At Somersby there was the whole dotty tribe of Tennysons, and Foxe, who wrote the terrifying *Book of Martyrs*, was rector of Boston.

Not that one had to be in orders to suffer from melancholia: Lincolnshire's landscape painter, Peter de Wint, while beginning each day with a prayer of thanksgiving usually ended it sunk in despondency. John Clare, a native of the fens, wrote most of his poetry while locked up in an asylum. William Cowper we can hardly claim as our own as he lived across the Wash in Norfolk, but he was depressed throughout his life and his gentle madness gave rise to those splendid lugubrious hymns so beloved of Mrs Belton.

Perhaps this melancholia arose from being latter-day Victorians: death had not yet been exchanged for sex as the main interest in life. We had three, widowed Poucher great-aunts, forever clad in black with their faces shrouded in delicate hat veils that were gathered at the throat by broad 'goitre bands' of moiré silk. Because of their widow's weeds, flutteringly agitated manner and sepulchral conversation, they were named by my sisters respectively 'Signs', 'Symptoms' and

...She wore shoes always too large

'Death': a trio of agelasts. Together they presented a terrifying aspect, but individually I found them approachable, if not exactly lovable. 'Signs' was Great-aunt Rachel, who gave us chocolate cake and allowed us to play her roulette wheel. She once lent my mother an umbrella with which to walk home in the rain. She walked a few paces before opening it, whereupon a shower of dead moths fell from the disintegrating interior and with the help of the increasing downpour glued themselves to my mother's hair, hat and coat.

'Symptoms' suffered from *petit-mal* and would 'go vacant' for short periods. 'Death', her sister, was endearingly odd and wore her shoes on the wrong feet, with the strap buttons over the instep and not on the outside of the foot. When together, their thin, high Gyrwie voices sounded like a pensive lament for the imaginary ailments of their family and friends. In true Edwardian fashion they dropped their 'g's and talked of 'sufferin' ' and 'dyin' ' and aspirated their 'h's to speak of 'evrah Sundah'. All three came from a tiny hamlet deep in the fens called Tanvats, a place of remote and desolate fascination.

The road to Tanvats lay across Metheringham Fen, a sodden

landscape perforated by drainage dykes and marked, at Sots Hole, by the only feature for miles around in the shape of a small copse, a refuge for pheasants. Under the immense sky the little community lay, where the road ended, huddled on the edge of the dyke – two farms and a row of farm cottages, some outbuildings and, dominating all, a sombre, red-brick Methodist chapel and a smaller schoolhouse alongside. Here the Pouchers and their farm workers laboured in the sugar beet and potato fields, set eel traps and shot wild-fowl. A greater contrast with the comfortable landscape of the wolds could not be imagined, which is perhaps one reason why my mother never wanted to visit her Poucher relatives at Tanvats. Indeed, I was only taken there once in my childhood – by one of my Dunham uncles who had married a Poucher. Beside their red cheeks, dark hair, long noses and slender figures with their keening voices, my squat, unsmiling Dunham uncle seemed almost an interloper. They gave us great slabs of fat bacon with

... A trio of agelasts

chutney and onions to eat, washed down with thick, dark tea. Pipes were lit and curtains drawn against the empty evening sky. When the time came to go home an ancient horse was saddled up and, storm lantern in hand, our host led us along the path beside the dykes to the beginning of the road.

If it was partly the landscape that kept people's spirits sombre, so was the constipating diet of pork and potatoes that contributed to their ponderous and sardonic humour. But jokes were few. I can recall only one that might be considered indigenous. My father had been told it by a farmer's wife that morning in the market and it was repeated by him at lunchtime.

'Nah then, meyster!' she greeted him in a loud voice that carried over the sheep pens, 'Dost thou know – ah, why lavatories 'ave no furniture in 'em?' Startled, my father replied that he did not, to which she replied, 'Becos' the Bums are allus' in!'

My father was not so much shocked by the story as he was by the farmer's wife presuming on an acquaintance she thought sufficiently close to permit her telling it to him. It was recounted not to amuse but to lead us to some understanding of the common law and debt. 'Bum' bailiffs (to distinguish them from farm managers also called bailiffs) we learnt were men who, acting on a magistrate's order, would constrain a person's goods and chattels for non-payment of debt. The pun in the conundrum remains lodged in a recess of memory. As an example of dour humour it might have appealed to Burton, who seemed otherwise unaffected by the youthful laughter that echoed through our house in Bridge Street.

When I was about three years old Burton left us and was replaced by our beloved Kathleen Belton. The first time she saw me, she wrote not long ago, I was eating a boiled egg with toast fingers, a sight which apparently did not deter her, for she stayed with us for years. Evidently the egg was generously distributed on and beyond the oilcloth bib which I wore round my neck. I remember the bib; it bore an illustrated nursery rhyme, 'Tom, Tom, the piper's son, stole a pig and away he run.' Was this a reminder of the ravaging in the fourth century of the Picts and Scots sweeping south to our prosperous and well-stocked lands?

... I was eating boiled egg with toast fingers

In due course Kathleen was joined by her mother and father in our employ and, later, by Eric their son, an heroic figure in both reality and in my imagination. The Belton family seems in retrospect to have been inseparable from ours – which was just as well, for very shortly after she had joined us, Kathleen's presence of mind saved me from an early and watery grave.

The lower warehouse, as it was called, had at one time served as a soft drinks plant owned by my grandfather Poucher. There, the green glass bottles were filled with such carbonated delights as lemonade, perry and a remarkable drink called 'Dandelion and Burdock', and then sealed with a glass ball in the neck. 'D & B' was reputed to be restorative and invigorating. The effluent from the plant was discharged by a drain directly into the river Bain as it flowed by our garden. The water steps, forbidden to me at that age, always beckoned, and one day Jane showed me where the drain came out. To see meant standing on the bottom step, clinging to the iron stanchion and craning my neck to look along the wall where the rambler roses tumbled in profusion into the water.

Holding on tightly, I could just see the drain outlet. No one, however, had noticed that Muriel and Kathleen were out in the canoe and, as neither could swim, had tied a clothes-line to the painter in case they needed to haul themselves back. This failsafe device was hitched not to the stanchion or the barge mooring ring, but to the bolt of one of the gates across the water steps. As I peered, the canoe paddled away beyond the elderberry bushes and out of sight. The line tightened. The gate gently swung to behind me and swept me headfirst into the river.

Someone shouted to my father that I was drowning and he flung off his coat and waistcoat and dashed to my rescue. Meanwhile, Kathleen and Muriel, round the bend in the river and unaware of what they had unwittingly caused, laughed with surprise when they spotted my new straw hat with its red ribbon sailing serenely downstream towards them. They attempted to retrieve it as it went by and were horrified to find that I was underneath it. Quickly undoing the painter they hotly pursued the hat and rescued me and it without tipping over the canoe.

This event is securely buried in my subconscious and it never lessened the attraction of the water steps. The full face of horror when it did appear was terrifying enough to keep me not only from the river but from the garden and the yard as well. For a long time afterwards the only way I could bring myself to enter the yard was by walking backwards to stop myself catching sight of what lay beyond the river bank.

On the opposite side of the Bain from our warehouses was a huddle of buildings owned by Nunkie Brown. An eccentric and a hoarder (as was later discovered) of gold, it was his indistinct speech, mimicked by me, that had given rise to a well-deserved beating. He was also a numerologist, accurately predicting the years of war, flood and other Malthusian disasters. I visited him often, taking our family's and others' bicycles to have punctures mended or fresh supplies of carbide put in the riding lamps. Nunkie possessed a donkey engine which he used to recharge motor car batteries and, in due course, wireless batteries – as there was no other source of energy for early radios.

Halcyon days were spent by us children in our walled garden by the river with the cascading roses, and where the tortoises, waggling their reptilian necks patrolled the four corners. It was an enchanted place, guarded by a stone lion set over the gateway, from which hung a great curtain of ivy and virginia creeper. Beyond the water steps my father had built a kind of folly – a high rockery of curiously carved pieces of limestone from his native Gloucestershire, in which were set winding paths bordered with long-necked green bottles from the defunct soda pop factory.

On very hot days we would put up a small, striped awning. I loved the mildew smell of the canvas – which still evokes childhood memories wherever the musty scent asserts itself. My mother would send Kathleen out with cooling bracelets of cucumber rind. Carefully peeled, they were slipped over the wrists where the veins came close to the skin. But my mother herself rarely came into the garden; the place lost its charm for her when a sycamore was planted instead of the copper beech on which she had set her heart.

Playing in this tranquil garden, and venturing forth from time to time to the top of the water steps to watch the river slide by, was to be part of a serene and utterly secure world. Nunkie's donkey engine punctuated the passing day. Its exhaust pipe rose above his workplace and, bent at right angles at the top with a flange at the end, it puffed away blackening the brick wall against which it rested. 'Puff, puff-puff puff, puff-puff' it went tirelessly on and on and there was no more friendly or comforting sound in the whole world.

One day, alone in the enclosed garden, I looked across at my ever-present companion and watched with mounting horror as the familiar exhaust pipe stirred, then began to move. Very slowly it turned from its resting place against the brick wall and settled its sightless gaze upon me. Blue fumes wreathing its dragon head, it coughed, 'Puff, puff, PUFF, puff, puff PUFF.' I screamed and fled into the yard, to be swept up by my father, into whose shoulder I buried my head. Belton appeared, with a hatchet at the ready; Kathleen rushed out of the kitchen. Tommy, the yardman, grabbed a shovel and my brothers dropped what they were doing. I do not know how they divined what had happened. Had they heard the change in rhythm of the engine? Later it transpired that the exhaust pipe had shifted because down below in his cabin Nunkie had fitted a new gasket and, in tightening it with a wrench, had turned the pipe away from the wall until its aperture faced across the river. My father's efforts to persuade me that there was nothing to be afraid of were in vain as, with my arms locked tightly round his neck, I struggled to hide my head in his coat. Belton had one of his 'turns' and eventually Kathleen led me back into the house.

I shunned the garden and the yard after that – for the river bank had fallen under the dominance of Nunkie's dragon. But I knew that they were there, golden in the afternoon sun, lapped by the water and guarded by my surrogates, the tortoises, until my return. Which was even more delayed, for I now fell prey to the usual childhood complaints and was soon down with either measles or scarlet fever. Terrified though I had been by Nunkie's dragon, I was never frightened by natural phenomena, except that one summer when I was ill and disturbed by the rolling thunder of distant storms. My sisters reassured me by insisting that the heavy rumbling was caused by the brewer's drayman rolling beer barrels up Mrs Pinkett's yard. Mrs Pinkett was the diminutive landlady of the Saracen's Head – that is, the dram shop down the street, not the one in Lincoln much frequented on market day by my great-grand-father, 'Booty' Dunham, and later by his son, Great-uncle Alf. To the shop, every few months or so, the brewer's dray would come from Newark in Nottinghamshire. The empties would roll down the yard, to be replaced by the deeper rumbling of the full ones as they made their way to the taproom. This accomplished, the two pairs of huge Clydesdales would tug at their traces and the great dray would move on.

My peaceable kingdom was bounded on one side by the Saracen's Head yard, where precious elastic bands could be salvaged from the discarded tops of stout bottles, and the river Bain with the garden on the other. At our back, beyond the warehouses, granary, stables, coal and ash houses, the river wound behind banks of elders and willows to the water mill.

Opposite, in a cottage by the river, lived the Beltons. Next door to them was a fish and chip shop owner who borrowed coal from us against the vision of the royalties he confidently anticipated from the patent then pending for his mechanical sugar beet lifter, cleaner, topper and tailer. The blueprints of this Heath Robinson device were contained in the bundle of papers he carried everywhere. The sugar beet lifter has long been a familiar feature of the Lincolnshire landscape in autumn and I wish there was some report that this sad-eyed scrounger had had a share in its development.

The summer had ended by the time I was convalescent, and it was too cold to remain long in the attic playroom. In the sitting room on the floor below, where the fireplace was larger and the room sunnier, I read whatever the shelves had to offer by way of history and adventure. There was a week or two to go before the prince set out on his winter travels, so together we plodded round the town, mapping the Roman wall which I had seen daily for most of my life without ever being aware of its presence or significance. Short stretches of it were still standing, the remnants of a horseshoe-shaped defence protected on the open side by the curve of the river Bain. It was built of massive stone, blackened now with age and moss and where it joined the river at the back of our stables it was covered in summer by a grapevine which ran from its roots in the river across the warehouse to the granary. Now that the leaves had fallen we could see where it had been strengthened by the Romans at a later date to mount their artillery. We traced the wall from further up in the town in Dog Kennel Yard, a place, we were told, where the mastiffs kept for baiting in the Bull Ring were housed. We lost it after that, but picked it up again in St Mary's Square by the hangman's shop where Hogg, the cobbler, mended shoes. It was difficult to follow beyond that point but a fragment came to view near where the Roman maze had been at the junction of the three rivers.

On the last day before he left us for the winter, the prince suggested that as Belton had just freshly dug the garden and a lot of topsoil would have washed down from the beds in the morning's rain, we should search for coins; if any were to be found they would be lying on the surface. The technique, he explained, was to wear a hat to shade the eyes, and to keep the eyes down *at all times*, so as not to miss anything. Thus blinkered we went, with my gaze riveted on my boots. After an hour we found six Roman coins, which I have before me now. They are from the reigns of the Emperors Licinius and Constantine I and II.

On a cold, clear day many years later in Libya, a self-appointed guide at Lepcis Magna (from where Septimus Serverus had come to rule Britain), led me unerringly to a Byzantine potsherd lying just below the surface of the sand. It only then occurred to me that the prince, too, might have had our excavation 'salted'. I had noticed, but failed to note, that my brother Harold, whose round-eyed drollery made him a highly skilled emissary for commissions of this kind, had indeed been closeted with the prince on some private matter about the time the skies had begun to lift after the rain. But it did the trick. Even if I was reluctant to look it in the eye, I no longer quailed before the indifferent gaze and hostile bark of the donkey engine exhaust. That false friend, treacherous companion and transpontine dragon, if not slain exactly, had been thoroughly scotched. The garden was repossessed and the way to the water steps lay open.

The prince almost gilded the lily. He produced from the poacher's pocket inside his Norfolk jacket two faded lettuce leaves, one each for Poley and Poley. For us he had tucked away two sticks of liquorice stuffed with Kali sherbet (for which he had developed a taste when living in Turkey) and sealed with pink sprinklers. We four then celebrated in the summerhouse while the sycamore leaves began to fall all around us and the rain dripping from the eaves washed the mud from off our treasure trove.

...while the sycamore leaves began to fall

SIX

'Some Village-Hampden'

... next to the newly install telephone

*T*he rumour that my father was a German spy surfaced suddenly in Horncastle in the summer of 1914. The dire news reached him by way of Miss Heaton, a well-to-do spinster friend of my parents. She had learned of it while crossing the Market Place from a knot of belligerent townsfolk who, as she later put it, 'At that very moment were gathering to smash the bakery windows in protest'. The Kaiser's agents were commonly supposed to be lurking everywhere, and window-breaking of the premises of those whose names or accents were unfamiliar was rife for a few days after the outbreak of the Great War, and constituted a popular if irresponsible way of venting feelings of misplaced patriotism.

Miss Heaton arrived at our house in a state of great agitation. Normally rather fluttery and nervous, her agitation increased as she had to sit and watch my father quietly finishing his tea. Eventually to her enormous relief he got up, put on his hat and strolled out round the corner to the Market Place. There he greeted what by this time was the beginnings of an unruly mob and immediately singled out the ring-leader – a pork butcher and a well-known frequenter of the Saracen's Head. He went straight up to him and with studied politeness, but in tones that all could hear, invited his opinion on a variety of inconsequential matters: the state of the fishing; the prospects for the local walking match; and whether, under the circumstances, the town gala and gymkhana should be held. A few people on the fringe of the crowd sloped off in the direction of the High Street, others seeing their leader thus addressed stopped grumbling and pressed closer to hear what was being said. The pork butcher, red-faced and spluttering, only got two or three words out before my father, to the astonishment of the onlookers, thrust his arm firmly through his protagonist's and marched him off across the Market Place and along Bridge Street to the doorway of the Saracen's Head. No more was heard about German spies.

While doubtless over the years the story improved with the telling, it does give some indication of the reserve with which my father was viewed by the townsfolk, as well as something

... thrust his arm firmly through his protagonist's

of his own robust spirit. He had married into a family and a county in which he never felt entirely at home. He was a product of the gentler ways of the West of England, never losing his native Gloucestershire burr: a sharp contrast to the dour manner and blunt speech of his Lincolnshire relatives-by-marriage.

My father was born in Tewkesbury in one of a row of medieval houses close to the Abbey, where my grandfather, Nelson Townley, was a stocking maker. Father held a striking resemblance to his older second cousin, Edward Elgar, and, apart from looking alike, in their early lives they had much in common. Elgar came from Worcester a few miles away, where his father had a music shop. Both participated in the liturgical music of Worcester Cathedral and Tewkesbury Abbey respectively, although Elgar was a Roman Catholic and my father in due course became a Quaker.

The memory of my father is always evoked for me by Elgar's

music, particularly in the pastoral passages: both the music and the man being vigorous and emphatic, full of charm and dignity and saved from rhythmic monotony by a puckish sense of humour surfacing at unlikely moments.

In his youth my father must have been something of a 'masher'. As a soldier in the territorial battalion of the Lincolnshire Regiment his uniform fitted him like a glove. He affected high collars, silk neckties and a *boutonnière*. Throughout his life I never saw him in casual clothes, always a suit, and he wore hard collars which, after his death, lasted me for several years. He was never encased, as were most men of his generation, in heavy long underwear. His moustaches were luxuriant and, in his youth, probably waxed. He was saved from looking like a haberdasher's apprentice on a bank holiday by his high, round forehead, firm chin with a deep cleft, erect, alert carriage and exceptionally powerful build. Later in life, while always correct and formal in his dress, he became indifferent to it, and his annually purchased suit was acquired for reasons other than that of sartorial splendour.

Solomon eclipsed? Maybe, for the early photographs reveal someone arrayed as the lilies of the field. His topper, still in use a generation later, was, as he put it, 'the cheapest hat I ever bought'. He was fond of the work of the New England essayist and wit Oliver Wendell Holmes and kept one of his books, *The Poet at the Breakfast Table*, by his bedside. He must have taken good counsel from him:

> Wear a good hat: the secret of your looks
> Lives with the beaver in Canadian brooks.
> Virtue may flower in an old cravat,
> But man and nature scorn a shocking hat.

But this was well before my time. It belonged to the era of my mother's courtship. Then, elaborate and thoughtful love letters were exchanged in immaculate copperplate, heavily housed – rather like my mother's watercolours – in the black-edged letter paper used by an empire indulging itself in prolonged mourning for Queen Victoria. In later years this breadth of style with the touch of gallantry was never lost. It shone through the debates on how to defeat the brewer, abolish the drainage rate, disestablish and disendow the Church of England, do away with the death penalty, give self-government to India and, above all, smash the shrine to Our Lady Nicotine.

The espouser of unpopular causes is not one to be surrounded by friends or be the most comfortable of neighbours. My father's critical and independent mind led him to prolonged spiritual searchings, which ended in unwavering decisions. Not that he was incapable of compromise: given the chance to play the organ in a local church he would hurry off with his hymnal under his arm. For the lessons he would descend from the organ and stand under the pulpit, one hand cupped behind an ear. Principles set aside, yes; but scruples, never. If offered a fee he would accept and put it in the poor box. He campaigned ceaselessly against the local drainage rate. Horncastle was the occasional victim of flash floods, as heavy collections of rain water in the northern wolds would disgorge themselves through the narrow waterways of the town, bringing high, almost instantaneous flooding. As the hill farmers reduced their ditches and tree cover to make larger fields, so the uninterrupted run-off from them became even more sudden and devastating to the downstream dweller. Ostensibly to pay for a controlled water regimen, a substantial tax was levied on the householder living below flood level. The drainage rate, introduced after the great flood of 1920, became an obsession with my father – so much so that he neglected what my mother considered to be more urgent matters.

There was about my father an innocent, spiritual primitiveness that would have found a home among the saints of the mid-seventeenth century: the Lollards, Diggers, Ranters, Fifth Monarchist Men, Levellers, Anabaptists, Familists, Mortalists, Seekers, Children of Light and Muggletonians, all were grand masters of the art of disapproval. With the exception of the Quakers, little remains of the social and spiritual ferment of that period. But the thread of evangelical fervour is still part of the good broadcloth of English life. Being neither a team player nor a 'joiner', my father exercised private philanthropy and the individual protest. Thus he did his stint as chairman of the local Liberal constituency party, the British and Foreign Bible Society, the Anti-Slavery and Aborigine Protection Society, and for a time was a reluctant poor law guardian. But he eschewed official life and was even unwilling to become an honorary member of the Old Rasputin Restoration Society.

His charity was personal and impromptu, and was almost indistinguishable from the conduct of his daily business, to the occasional consternation of my mother and the amazement of her relatives. Indeed, it could become quite complicated, as when supporting a nation's decision to go to war he felt, nevertheless, that he should not profit by it. (It is very difficult for a successful businessman not to accumulate a fortune in wartime.) I sometimes felt, as I grew older, that he would have been happier with a mighty cause, with a vision of a New Jerusalem. My sense of the immediacy of history must spring, I think, from my growing up with the distinct impression that the revocation of the Edict of Nantes had occurred not in 1685 but just a few weeks before I appeared on the scene. The struggle of the Hugenots was a subject often discussed, although whether my father would have passed muster with those Calvinists or they with him is moot. Although not a monarchist, he had a soft spot for the Stuart kings, his favourites among them being James I, who pamphleteered against 'that pernicious weed', the tobacco plant, and Charles II who made the land grant to the Quaker William Penn for his 'holy experiment' in the New World. He would have welcomed the ideals from which grew the Civil War in England, but not the military rule that followed.

The Puritan leader who most excited imagination was John Hampden because of his opposition to 'Ship Money'. This was a tax imposed by Charles I without the authority of Parliament that led to the Civil War in which Hampden was to die in 1643 from wounds received in battle. As children we all enjoyed reciting the first stanza of Thomas Gray's 'Elegy written in a Country Churchyard', if only to see in how many ways Jane could rearrange the line:

The ploughman homeward plods his weary way.

89

Later in the poem Gray soliloquizes on who might lie buried there:

> Some village-Hampden, that with dauntless breast
> The little tyrant of his fields withstood;
> Some mute inglorious Milton here may rest,
> Some Cromwell guiltless of his country's blood.

My father was a would-be Hampden. But in my childhood at least, the measures needed to eradicate social injustice and to lift the country out of its economic morass did not require the heroic posture of those seventeenth-century seekers after Grace Abounding.

As did many other countries, England lived under the lengthened shadow of the Great War. In our immediate circle survivors included a favourite uncle wounded at Loos, Belton so badly gassed at Ypres, and the upholsterer for whom my father provided a workshop in one of our warehouses. He had a wooden leg and used to terrify my schoolmates by casually taking a tack from his mouth and tapping it into his leg to keep his sock up. The aftermath of the war affected the lives of everyone, but perhaps less so of those who lived in remote country areas, cut off from the events that were transforming the rest of British society. In our relatively still backwater we were reminded of the mainstream by only an occasional eddy.

One obvious social change was the coming of the motor car to rural areas. The first was the Model A Ford, or 'Tin Lizzie', which was soon replaced because it was too big for rolling English roads, by the 'Baby' Austin and the Morris Eight. In our large family, however, our 'Tin Lizzie' was replaced by a Standard Ten and eventually the George-Marina.

We took the one daily newspaper that my father considered did not express the megalomania of its proprietor and, in the thirties, the wireless arrived with popular programmes. Soon Frank's crystal set, that to the delight of the prince could pick up Radio Tiflis, was replaced by a radio in an ornate, highly polished walnut case which stood in the corner of the downstairs parlour next to the newly-installed telephone. By

90

means of this latest piece of technology we could now be in instant touch with relatives in far-flung Gloucestershire or Derbyshire. To obtain a number, either locally or long distance, one picked up the black, bakelite daffodil mouth-piece, clamped the listening part on the end of a long, curly flex to the ear, and waited for the voice of a Poucher cousin who manned the Horncastle switchboard to request the number. The silent pictures, and eventually the 'talkies' came, but in Horncastle they nearly did not. When the Corn Exchange, where my family did so much of its business was converted into a cinema, my father witheld his share of the promised investment unless at least half the seats were reserved for non-smokers.

It was probably all these improvements in home life that kept people out of the public houses, rather than the remonstrations of my father and others. His views on drink anyway might not have been all that strong. He was happy to sup cider with the Elgars at their house in Hereford, or when visiting farming cousins in Gloucestershire. Nevertheless, he felt that Horncastle had an excessive number of dram shops, even though they were mainly to slake the gargantuan thirst of a small town swollen once a year by the influx for the Horse Fair.

Father's vigorous, cheerful and outgoing manner must have served him in good stead as he ordered drunks home to their wives and separated the Irish who were given to fighting one another for what remained of their pay packets after closing time on a Saturday night. Tough but softspoken men, they came every year towards the 'back-end' for the heavy and demanding labour of beet pulling and potato picking. Such seasonal, migrant labour he treated with great kindness and consideration, as he did the miners when they came – almost as if they were a people set apart for whom normal rules did not apply.

After the Elgars, the Irish were the only Catholics tolerated. Father's religious bigotry was shared by the rest of us. We were familiar with the horrible sights of the Inquisition illustrated in Foxe's *Book of Martyrs*. It never occurred to us that the persecuted turns on his persecutors and, in the interests of

91

religious tolerance, can treat with equal severity those who seek similar freedom of worship. My father's Quaker belief was simple and unadorned: if God is to be worshipped in spirit and in truth no intermediary is required; God is present within each of us. Lest this should lead to spiritual anarchy, there was the Bible to keep us faithful and provide a record of His purpose for all men.

Such a faith is exacting in practice. It becomes more so when all props and stays are discarded. The rejection of all forms, rites, symbols and observances meant the structure, too, had to come from within, and this, being demanding, led to some degree of isolation. But there were occasions when my father's anti-clericalism, seemingly rigid, would emerge in playful tone. He delighted in the story of 'Booty' Dunham and his nieces' marriages. My great-grandfather, 'Booty' Dunham, being an unpretentious woolbacker, was not entirely pleased at the sight of them being courted by a pair of curates with uncertain futures. Returning home early one Friday from Lincoln market, he overheard on the train two gaitered divines discussing the disposal of nearby livings. Great-grandfather, enclogged and with his whistle thoroughly wetted, continued with them on the train to London. Once there, he followed the two reverend gentlemen to Church House. After assuaging any anxieties his unprepossessing appearance and manner may have caused, he bought on the spot two of the livings for six hundred guineas each. Having had a successful day at the market he was able to count from his money bags twelve hundred gold sovereigns and on arrival back in Lincolnshire he presented the livings to his nieces as dowries.

The marriages took place. Whereupon social airs were acquired; both clergymen promptly hyphenated their names; they smoked large, curved calabash pipes, wore the newly-fashionable 'boater' and learned to enjoy the pleasures of the table. Apart from occasional contact, they passed from our ken. It was either hyphenated-Brown or hyphenated-Smith who wrote to my mother on becoming an archdeacon many years later and reminded her that the correct form of address to him was no longer 'Reverend' but 'The Venerable'. Henceforth, unknowingly, he was always referred to by us as 'the Venereal Archdeacon'. There were no parental remonstrances.

The rhythmic monotony of my father's utterances, however, rose to a threnody when he turned to the subject of tobacco. The sight of nicotine stains on the fingers of someone asking for his support, financial or otherwise, would leave the unsuspecting supplicant bewildered – although ultimately rewarded. He was concerned, not with the health hazards of smoking (which were then unknown) but with the eroding effect on a family's budget and, perhaps, too, exasperation at what to him was the ludicrous sight of a man sucking on a substitute nipple and claiming it as a symbol of manhood. Similarly, my father's support, such as it was, for the temperance movement arose from witnessing only too often the impoverishment of the drunkard's family, and on that ground alone he waged a personally expensive war of attrition against brewer and distiller alike.

But if we were not saved from bigotry we were preserved from priggishness by my father's bluff and humorous complacency, buttressed by a certain lethargy that occasionally seemed to overwhelm him, to the relief of us all.

As every child knows, however, the influence of a father upon his children is not derived from what he says, but by how he lives. Personally frugal, he considered his wants were met when he accompanied my mother on an annual shopping expedition to Lincoln. He made two purchases. Clutching whatever book he was currently reading, he would repair down the Cornmarket to F. W. Woolworth and Company 3d and 6d Stores and there work along the counter containing racks of steel-framed reading glasses. He would try on every pair until he found one that suited him, and would then match that pair to others with identical lenses. He would then purchase the lot, being somewhat prodigal in his use of them. The next stop was just above the Stonebow – the sixteenth-century gateway already much given to obstructing traffic, dividing the 'above hill' from the 'below hill' of Lincoln – where at his tailor he would be joined by my mother for the purpose of ordering a new suit. His clothing went unremarked and, indeed, unnoticed by us children. He always asked the

... He would try on every pair

tailor for 'the same again' – for he saw no reason to change either the texture, style or cut. The wool came from the backs of our own Lincolnshire Longwools; it was woven in the same Bradford mills in which our family had an interest; and it was made up by the same tailor, who offered a small discount. My mother, I think, always wished to find something different. I cannot, however, remember my father wearing anything but a three-piece suit of Quaker grey, narrow in the trouser, cut high in the waistcoat and full-skirted in the coat.

The final call, before leaving for Horncastle, was tea with 'Spider' Birkett, clerk of Lincoln Meeting (of the Society of Friends) and headmaster of a local school. His house, perched high on the limestone ridge by the castle, looked down on the racecourse where, in March, the flat-racing season would open with the Lincolnshire Handicap. But this was January, and by tea-time it was dark. Restored by home-made shortbread and Dundee cake my parents would receive from Mrs Birkett hot bricks wrapped in flannel to put under their feet in the car.

Then they would drive back over the snow-drifted wolds, the bitter north-east winds cutting through the flapping side-curtains of the vehicle. These homeward rides were often the only journeys they would take alone together during the year, for on the way in to Lincoln they were usually accompanied by Great-uncle Alfred Dunham. Half an hour before they were due to set out, great-uncle's evening clothes in a large leather grip would be brought up on a wheelbarrow by the ever-faithful Mackinder and put in the boot of the car, together with a securely locked Gladstone bag.

Suckled as my mother and her forebears had been at the iron breast of Wesleyan Methodism, the atavistic craving for ritual and symbolism, so firmly suppressed in their religious observances, found its way into the lives of my mother's uncles and cousins through masonic rites. These gruff and taciturn men found nothing unusual in donning funny aprons and other bits and pieces of secret regalia in which at stated intervals they indulged in harmless if obscure rites. Such practices were a source of embarrassment to my mother, of tolerant amusement to my father, and of endless and hilarious mimicry for us children. As always, my father sought to allay my mother's distress in such matters and partially reassured her by stating that masonry had its origins in the anti-clerical movement, and that one of our family's heroes, Garibaldi, had been a freemason.

So, if the Lincoln visit coincided with Lodge Night, Great-uncle Alf would be taken and dropped at the Saracen's Head at the bottom of Cornhill, where for several generations his family had conducted their business at Lincoln Market. As my mother would not allow her uncle to smoke in the car she supplied him with a bag of Quincy's butterscotch, made at Louth. Being stone deaf, he was quite unaware of the sucking and crunching noises he made, which were so loud that, much to my father's irritation, they precluded any conversation. Once at the Saracen's Head, he would settle himself in the Snug, nursing a small whisky, his evil pipe billowing clouds of shag, the battery of his hearing aid freshly charged. There ensconced, he would talk wool prices with fellow merchants and the more well-to-do woolbackers until it was time to dress, unlock his regalia from the Gladstone bag and sally forth to the lodge of which he was a past master.

After 1930 these journeys to Lincoln came to an end – for a reason that we all welcomed, because it was then that my father ceased to be a poor law guardian.

A hundred years before, the New Poor Law came into effect. Its guiding principle was that poverty was wayward-ness. Parishes were grouped into 'unions' and in market towns such as ours, barracks to house the poor were built. The gentler provision of 'outdoor relief' was abandoned: for the pauper it was the workhouse or nothing. In these Dickensian horrors spouses were separated and under the eye of the workhouse master a harsh and humiliating discipline was enforced. This system, designed to encourage the able-bodied to move and take to the roads to find work, was overseen by locally appointed poor law guardians and was still in operation at the time I was a child. The union – as the workhouse came to be named – provided bed and board for a hopeless jumble of the crazed, the ancient, the incapacitated, the waif and the helpless, while the country roads were full of tramps plodding from one union to another, ostensibly in search of work. I soon developed a liking for these unkempt persons who would emerge from the hedgerows and greet my father with 'Nah then, meyster!' Later, they would appear at the side door to ask for a bread loaf – to which was usually added a couple of slabs of fat bacon or a lardy cake.

We shared with our father the distress he felt in having assumed this one civic duty: no more so than on Christmas Day. By the time the first of the roast turkey smells began to seek us across the yard, my father had quietly left – for he took it upon himself each Christmas to carve the geese for the inmates of the workhouse. We would wait for what to us seemed an endless time. When he returned, my mother always went out to meet him, and together, without a word to us children, they retired upstairs, my father looking strangely diminished, indeed, defeated. After another long wait my mother would come downstairs first, like a votive goddess bearing in her arms my father's clothes. 'We won't be long, children, Kathleen, you may dish up and Frank, you had better carve,' she would say as she passed through the kitchen and scullery into the washhouse. There, with a fastidiousness that matched all her movements, she lowered my father's shirt and collar into the copper. The suit she fed into the furnace.

The last suit my father bought was the one made for him in 1930. That year, local government acts abolished the poor law guardians. The law governing eye glasses was also changed and precluded their sale without prescription. Frank, now twenty, drove Great-uncle Alfred to his Lodge Nights. The burning of the suit on Christmas Day can now be seen not so much as a matter of hygiene, but as a rite of cleansing, of expiation, an offering, a symbolic act of witness and a renewal of hope.

... *one made for him in 1930*

SEVEN

Foolish Fires

... *he rose majestically into the saddle*

*T*here was one deep-seated difference between my father's and my attitudes. It lay in his healthy disregard for grandiloquent global systems, upon the elaboration and perfection of which I had set my heart and what little head I then possessed. In fact, my father's view of causes, particularly those which were the object of his own philanthropy, had something akin to the hallmark of the civil servant who refrains from absolute commitment to whatever his current governors have decided to pursue. For who knows what the morrow may bring? Perhaps my father's attitude may best be set out in the way he approached the three causes with which, in some fit of absence of mind, he found himself lumbered.

The first of these was the British and Foreign Bible Society, and the Anti-Slavery and Aborigines Protection Society was another. Assiduous in his support of the former he was aware of its possible counter-productive results. A missionary exercise to flood with weighty Bibles a country having rather sketchy public services was bound to disrupt such government postal departments as might exist – as it had in fact done in Persia. Somewhat less was his enthusiasm for the Anti-Slavery and Aborigines Protection Society. But why did father support it at all – a body whose reputation lay firmly embedded in its past? Was it an act of expiation for Great-uncle Morton's association, when he was inspector-general of the Ottoman Bank, with Sultan Ahmed the Damned? According to the prince, when on a certain evening he returned rather unsteadily from a visit to the Morton household at Thimbleby Top, one of the reasons for great-uncle's periodic forays into the Caucasus was to purchase Circassian virgins for the seraglio. It was from those travels that Great-uncle Morton had become something of an *afficionado* of the *danse de ventre*. This, the prince explained, for our benefit, was taught by those mothers intent upon selling their daughters off at a high price. The dance, clumsily executed by the prince high-flown with cough medicine, was a means of demonstrating child-bearing capabilities, the movements being those of the act of parturition. We children would not have known.

The worldly cause, however, about which my father was most hesitant was the Society for the Propagation of the Christian Gospel among the Jews. Its aims seemed presumptuous, as if carrying coals to Newcastle. It was probably his friend the Reverend Isaacs who involved him in the Society. A character straight out of Trollope, the Reverend Isaacs, rector of Hemingby, a small and lovely village in the wolds, each Monday would ride into town on a high-frame bicycle. This he would leave in our care and catch the morning train that connected at Horncastle Junction with the London mail. Closeted in the British Museum all week, the rector reluctantly returned on Friday to spend the weekend giving perfunctory attention to the spiritual needs of his parishoners. So perfunctory, in fact, that he sometimes forgot to appear at weddings at which he had agreed to officiate.

On the Friday evening after taking tea with us, the Reverend Isaacs would retrieve his bicycle, mounting it by a rear step from which he rose majestically into the saddle. At the same moment he doffed his hat – a courtesy which required faultless timing and a steady nerve. Quite what the rector's standing in the diocese was, was something of a mystery. Although he did not wear the apron that would have become him as a rural dean, he did wear gaiters which bespoke the authority of an archdeacon. This we knew, from our distant relatives who were, that he was not. With the pragmatism of childhood we saw the gaiters as enabling the rector to pedal in greater comfort. But the puzzle remained unsolved.

One Friday the Reverend Isaacs asked my mother if she would be hostess to a missionary about to arrive on furlough from the Holy Land and who was, to boot, a high official of the Society. My father, when consulted, looked doubtful, for it meant that one of his chickens would be coming home to roost. For what was the point of such far-flung philanthropies if they could not be cultivated at a decent distance? My mother had to be assured on two counts. She would allow anybody and nearly anything into the house (the doors of which were never locked) except Catholic priests and Jerusalem artichokes. She feared he might be one and, coming from

Palestine, wish to be fed on the other. It was the sole vegetable that she found detestable.

The Reverend Isaacs reassured her as to the suitability of the sect, and my father in the matter of the artichokes. Nor need my father have worried. The purveyor of the Christian gospel had, amongst his disregarding flock, become completely absorbed in Talmudic scholarship and Hebrew tradition. He dressed as a rabbi, kept the Jewish Sabbath, wore a yarmulka and prayed wearing his phylacteries. Small, slender and dapper, gesticulating madly with a staccato but faultless delivery, the missionary, having become converted, ceased to convert. We loved him. He introduced us to Jewish belief, taught us some Hebrew and lifted the veil on the history of Israel. We treasure to this day the snuff box he presented to my mother, a somewhat incongruous present for a lady with such abstemious habits. But it was made of sweet-smelling wood from Solomon's cedars, was adorned with Hebrew texts and had a secret unlocking device: something for everyone.

Apart from these three distant obligations, my father firmly eschewed anything approaching a grand design. Perhaps he was mindful of William Blake – 'Whoever wishes to do good to his neighbour should do so on small occasions, for the general good is always invoked by scoundrels, hypocrites and flatterers.' So he remained, or so it seemed to me, stubbornly provincial, indeed parochial, in his charities, reflecting his *idées fixes*. But his views were neither archaic nor ignorant. They remain germane, even if the reasons for them are now quite different.

Disestablishment and disendowment of the Church of England, in his view, would provide a dramatic opportunity to renew and revitalize faith, perhaps leading to church unity. Furthermore, he had succumbed as he frequently did to the temptation to tease. As a business man, he felt that the clergy might with benefit be exposed to the economic winds that were blowing with increasing severity round the skirts of commerce. Could they not be paid by results, like coal miners? From such strictures, of course, his friend the rector of Hemingby was exempt. This benign if quirky approach to grave matters reached its peak one year in the case of the washhouse scrubbing table.

There was a small Roman Catholic community near Woodhall whose priest, in some trepidation, came over to call on my father. There was a need, he explained, to have somewhere to hear confessions and to say Mass for the Irish migratory labourers who came to Lincolnshire every autumn for the 'back-end', or second harvest. For these purposes he sought to rent the Liberal club each Sunday during this period. The conversation took place in the club, of which my father was chairman. He refused the request brusquely. As the crestfallen priest turned away my father added: 'How could I possibly have you pay rent? You must have the club free of charge.' My mother was not informed.

My father narrowly escaped his day of reckoning when, on the very first Sunday, the priest appeared at the washhouse door in a state of great perturbation, just as my brothers and I were cleaning our boots. He told us that the club billiard table was too big to serve as an altar. My father was surreptitiously summoned and the problem was resolved with the offer, promptly accepted, of the washhouse scrubbing table. It was furtively carried, on my father's instructions, across the Market Place to the clubroom. A condition of its loan was that it had to be returned before nightfall, otherwise all would be discovered when our clothes came to be left there in readiness for Monday morning. An additional condition was that the priest agree to debate publicly with my father the Catholic and Protestant views on transubstantiation. Clutching a loaf of day-old bread we had given him, the harassed priest agreed and hurried away.

Two months later, due to some oversight, the scrubbing table failed to reappear on the Sunday evening. The day of reckoning had indeed arrived. My brothers scuttled off to retrieve the table. When it regained the washhouse my mother scrubbed it vigorously to remove any trace of sacerdotal sacrilege of her domestic hearth. That night our scalps were examined with unaccustomed severity for any trace of nits. My father retired to his books. I learned that retribution when it falls is seldom evenhanded.

Then came the evening of the Great Debate. The Corn Exchange was filled to capacity with Catholics from Woodhall Spa, Quakers from Lincoln, and Methodists, Congregationalists and Anglicans from Horncastle. My mother's report of the evening was confusing. The Reverend Isaacs was in the chair. Apparently he thought the debate was on the fourth-century dispute over the nature of the Trinity. In a voice that was pitched to whispered exchanges in the reading room of the British Museum but barely audible in our Corn Exchange, the rector read from his latest work on the Council of Nicea. The audience became comatose, but was quickly roused by my father's opening 'Friends, Romans, Countrymen!' to the point where it became unruly. Seizing control of the meeting, he closed the proceedings by standing up and starting to sing the 'Old Hundredth', whereupon the relieved priest, bewildered Isaacs and turbulent Christians all thundered forth. Whatever the outcome, He from whom all blessings flow had emerged triumphant.

In spite of the periodic invasions into our bright household by an assortment of colonial cousins, visiting relatives from other parts of England, 'Spider' Birkett on the occasion of the Goose Fair and of course the annual visitation by the prince, we dwelt in comparative isolation which, turning us inward, limited us to local life and thought. We were never shaken by so much as a quiver of empirical uncertainty. We read newspapers, but in summertime only for the cricket. A wireless set came to replace Frank's cats-whisker crystal set that was retired to the Ark. We listened to highminded talks on the BBC and, on Saturday nights, to the music hall. My father would unbend sufficiently to join us if he could be assured that his favourite comedian, Nosmo King, was performing. (None of us could understand his quick-fire cockney Jewish drollery, but he was respected for having selected his stage name from the 'No Smoking' sign on a rapidly moving railway carriage.) The silent movies had arrived at the Corn Exchange, newly converted to a cinema, and I was, too infrequently, allowed to attend accompanied by Mrs Miller who did our heavy cleaning. She tended to deflate dramatic moments by anticipation: 'Look out! 'e's be-ind you!' she would shout at Tom Mix and, then towards the end after the heroine had been rescued 'Ah! In't that luvly, now 'e'm goin' to kiss 'er!'

These minor incursions into our little world did nothing to test our inoculation against the age of uncertainty. In music the diatonic scale came not near. Elgar was our norm; the nearest approach to modernism was the daring playing by our local amateur orchestra, some thirty years after its première, of Frederick Delius' *Brigg Fair*, possibly out of loyalty to a rather dreary, neighbouring market town of that name. 'More like Brigg Funeral' was the general comment. Cubism and Surrealism were unknown. We were still getting over Whistler 'charging two hundred guineas for flinging a pot of paint in the public's face', as Ruskin put it. Einstein, upsetting the order of our fellow yellow-belly Isaac Newton, left us unmoved, as did the revelations of that subterranean, ungovernable engine, the

... now e'm going to kiss 'er

subconscious, by Doctors Adler, Freud and Jung. New worlds of the written word opened up by Proust, Ezra Pound, James Joyce and T. S. Eliot did not budge us from our Ptolemaic view of life, literature and the arts. Although I do recall my father asking me whether I had ever seen an evening 'spread out against the sky like a patient etherized upon a table'. I kept looking.

Turning homewards, we came face-to-face, so to speak, with the poet who married the girl next door. After a long courtship Alfred Tennyson married Emily Sellwood whose older sister was already the wife of Sir John Franklin the explorer, from nearby Spilsby. The Tennysons were, as we say in Lincolnshire, a 'rum lot' and as like as not 'as daft as muck'. Their father, the rector of Somersby, a hamlet nestling in a fold of the wolds, was drunken, morose and violent. He fathered twelve children – some mad, all odd. Relatively sane, Alfred's youngest sister Emily was wont to open her umbrella in church to keep off the draughts, and their brother Septimus would greet visitors by rising from the floor on which he would be lying with the words 'I am Septimus, the most morbid of the Tennysons.' To cap it all, there was an uncle with pretensions to nobility who, as the French saying goes, 'trouvé son nom sur un tombeau' and tacked on d'Eyncourt to his name. He lived in an elaborately constructed gothic ruin and spoke of his nephew's poetry as, 'What do you expect of a hog but grunts?' Tennyson was, indeed, what my brothers would have termed 'a bit of a rough pup'. He smoked ploughman's shag, drank grocer's port, spoke with the heavy accents of the wold woolbacker, grumbled about money and put his foot in it wherever he went, particularly at court. This however endeared him to Queen Victoria who, in her widowhood, liked to have around her people more rough-hewn than the ever-to-be-mourned Prince Consort.

None of this reached our ears in those days, although the melancholy, the despair, the unrequited love, the dripping eaves and lost hopes of the poems convey something of an inner sadness of a childhood destroyed. But Tennyson's strength lay in his harsh landscapes illuminated by flashes of transcendental beauty. His poetry imparts a stoicism and an immovable confidence. Perhaps persistent pessimism is the price that absolute self-assurance always has to pay. For me, however, the chief pleasure lay in Tennyson's looking eastward to the sea. His shore poems, regardless of their solemnity, evoke all the salty, sandy Sundays of childhood, the silver sea and hissing tide foam that raced so fast across the flats to break short of the golden dunes. Not for us, however, were 'The Idylls of the King'. There was something not quite right about all those Arthurian knights weeping and swooning: not quite the thing. Robin Hood clad in Lincoln Green and Hereward the Wake down in the fens around Bourne never wept. It was Lombard Street to a blood orange they never did.

An unrelieved diet of Tennyson's massive Victorian confidence and solidity would be like spending one's life at Ghent or The Hague surrounded by solid worth and rich burgher houses. Happily, thanks to my father, I discovered Andrew Marvell. Like Tennyson, he was a poet, a parson's son and lover of his native Lincolnshire. But there the comparison ends. His poetry was the antidote to Tennyson's sanctimonious melancholy.

Not that metaphysical poets were my father's cup of tea. Far from it. He loved Tennyson, and the American Quaker hymnalist, John Greenleaf Whittier, and shared with the prince a liking for the poems of Thomas Hood. The latter endeared himself to us for a slightly unkind set of verses he wrote about the King's Champion. The Dymoke family at Scrivelsby Court had acquired by marriage the hereditary, but undemanding, title of King's Champion. It thus fell to successive members of that family to maintain the tradition of throwing down the gauntlet at the monarch's coronation banquet in Westminster Hall calling on any who wished to challenge the legitimacy of the royal title. Fortunately for the Champion, no one ever did, and with the accession of King William the Fourth the traditional ceremony was discontinued. However, in 1842 the young Queen Victoria created Mr Dymoke a baronet. Thus did Sir Henry Dymoke of Scrivelsby return his rented armour and go home to his pigs and poultry. Thomas Hood commemorated the event:

You toss in your breastplate your pancakes, and grow
A salad of mustard and cress in your helmet
. . . instead of your brow put beer in your casque.

A far cry from Andrew Marvell, born at Winestead in the
northern wolds overlooking the great estuary up which the
Eagre rolls when tides are neap:

To walk and pass our long love's day,
Thou by the Indian Ganges' side
Shouldst rubies find; I by the tide
Of Humber should complain. . .

Oh, Marvell was after my own heart – and head; a Cavalier by
taste and temperament, but a Roundhead by conviction and
duty. Mistakenly, I thought he had fought at the battle of
Naseby. When I reported on this, the prince, in a rare moment
of acerbity, enquired whether Marvell had fought on both
sides at once. In fact, Marvell did serve as tutor in the house of
Lord Fairfax, the Parliamentary general, and later as assistant
to John Milton when he was Latin Secretary to Oliver
Cromwell, a post which covered the correspondence and
conduct of foreign affairs.

It was not the career of distinguished public service in
turbulent times that interested me so much as the poetry. Here
was a gay-hearted lover, bubbling with high spirits, striving
hard to uncover the tangible if cruel beauty of country life in
everyday sights and sounds: a bee, a blade of grass, a dewdrop,
a nightingale. He sought a universal truth beyond nature's
wonders. He sought not only to admire but, in the spirit of
scientific enquiry, to examine and understand.

It was a railway timetable that eventually led my father to
Marvell. Father, before he married, at summer weekends
would take a train to Malvern or Hereford, with his bicycle
snug in the guard's van, where on arrival he would ride over to
see the Elgars. After some refreshment he would bicycle to
another station where another train would take him to his
brother's house for the night. Finally, by dint of his timetable,

... their phosphorescence illuminated the watch face

he would work his way across country back to his lodgings. Once, at dusk, he stopped to see what time it was, as the last train was due to leave in half an hour or so and he still had some ground to cover. Too dark to see, he laid his turnip watch on the grass verge. A minute passed and then the glow-worms appeared and their phosphorescence illuminated the watch face. And so to Marvell:

Ye living lamps by whose dear light
The nightingale does sit so late,
And studying all the summernight,
Her matchless songs does meditate.

Ye country comets that portend
No war nor prince's funeral,
Shining unto no higher end
Than to presage the grass's fall;
Ye glowworms, whose officious flame

To wandering mowers show their way,
That in the night have lost their aim,
And after foolish fires do stray;

I was captivated by Marvell's sharp-etched clarity and, in an untutored way, shared his quest for universal significance through an understanding of nature. I was convinced of the need to translate somehow the microcosm of our own secure lives into wider terms. Otherwise, the order in which we lived would be just as spurious as fairyland. How this was to be accomplished was not as yet clear, but I felt in my bones that my father's being kind, loving and understanding, lending and giving, simply was not enough. Our lives had to fit into a pattern that had universal validity. Moreover, I wanted the solution at once, with all the impatience of childhood. These speculations I explained to Hogg, the cobbler and my willing listener, who, with his mouth full of hobnails just nodded wisely at the prospect of my being turned into an instant theorem.

I neglected my routine school work and obligations, which gave rise to some watchful concern on the part of my brothers and sisters. Brown, from across the river, let me know that what was good enough for my father was good enough for him. George, the head baker, suggested shyly that it was as well to learn how to walk before learning how to run. Harold, a pragmatist in all matters, tried a diversion by teaching me how to bake horse chestnuts so that when the highly popular autumn game of 'conkers' began we would have an almost unassailable string to swing against the soft-fleshed ones of our opponents. But, to no avail, for I had loftier matters in hand. A Dunham uncle warned me of the dangers of flying too high.

To counter this, I produced my most cherished possession, the swagger stick given me by Eric when he had finished his period of service in the Royal Air Force. I pointed proudly to the *Per Ardua ad Astra* embossed on its silver knob. Support was also found (by accident, or design?) in the Reverend Isaacs. Wheeling the bicycle out of the shed for him when he returned one Friday from London I heard him say, to no one in particular:

> Ah, but a man's reach should exceed his grasp,
> Or what's a heaven for?

My father intervened in a way both canny and slightly devious, and with a significance not meant to be immediately apparent. In one or other of our bedrooms, except during periodic banishment to the attic, there hung a print of Holman Hunt's *The Light of the World*. About the time I was embarking on my cosmic quest, this piece of Victorian sentimentality had migrated to the wall at the foot of my bed. (It was, however, greatly to be preferred to *The Infant Samuel*.) One evening I found that the Holman Hunt had been replaced by a print of Pieter Breughel the Elder's *Landscape with the Fall of Icarus*.

In the foreground of the painting is a stolid Flemish peasant, looking remarkably like any one of my great-uncles. With a bland, expressionless gaze he continues to reap. Here is a man who never needed and never would need a glow-worm. He is no wandering mower who after foolish fires would stray. Is he entirely unaware that, in the far distance, a pathetic, naked figure is plunging, unheeded, to his doom in a tangle of broken hopes and melted wings?

... and in the far distance, a pathetic, naked figure is plunging

...the razor would flash

L etters were read at the breakfast table: newspapers never. An exception must have been the day when the *News Chronicle* announced that ex-President Calvin Coolidge had died. The circumstances of his death were that it took place at eleven o'clock in the morning while shaving. These did not call for comment, although the event, of course, did. My mother provoked the discussion by saying that Coolidge's widow, who was called Grace, had a lovely name. The prince added that President Coolidge, famous, notorious even, for the brevity of his utterances, would not have felt at home amidst our ceaseless chatter. My father thereupon went into a fairly substantial discourse on the inability of Americans to understand the nature of foreign debt. He concluded that the brusque rejoinder of President Coolidge when asked about the redemption of loans by France and Britain: 'They hired the money, didn't they?' would have been a remark worthy of our mother's Dunham uncles. At this, the prince, with the appearance of a hastily contrived afterthought, added that America was at last becoming a great power exhibiting already some of the basic characteristics of one including, what he termed, 'selective amnesia', for repudiation and default in the United States of state foreign debt had once been sufficiently frequent as to be almost customary.

To proceed to one's Maker while shaving in mid-morning, however, passed without notice. My father, after all, shaved at that time. Being out and about before seven, with breakfast at eight, followed by supervision in the yard and elsewhere, kept him busy for much of the morning until he came in, cleaned himself up and shaved. This was a period of ritual and relaxation. The razor of the day was selected and stropped. The hollow-ground steel sang or whinnied on the leather, depending on the side of the strop used. The ivory handle, now dark-yellow with age, nestled in my father's palm with the intimacy of long use. Then the pewter tankard would be filled from the copper hot water can. The silver mug had been discarded long ago – given to the prince quite likely – as it did not hold the heat, and the huge china one, chipped and stained, had been consigned to our attic treasures. Brush and soap followed with the texture of the latter exact in its viscosity. Later the razor would flash and the soap fall, from behind which, after two soapings, would emerge a pink, smooth, benign and refreshed father. If he had any time in hand he would soap himself extra heavily and then draw clown faces with his fingers through the soap to amuse us. The daily practice of shaving, however, was abandoned on Sundays when my mother required that all ablutions should be completed earlier because of the call of the Moslem.

There was a good reason for calling the upstairs sitting-room 'the Moslem'. It had, as it were, an almost infinite capacity for absorbing artifacts, without our ever having to remove anything. Nothing ever was, except, that is, for a Benares brass tray which my father discovered had been made in Birmingham. (It adorned Mrs Belton's parlour for many years afterwards.) And, of course, when the prince visited, the library steps. But these were the exceptions that proved the rule, for they were not removed to make space.

'Dear God, May!' exclaimed the prince once in mock dismay. 'You are turning this place into a mausoleum!' My mother beamed and replied, 'Of course, Vanya dear, after all we are all buried here!' From then onwards, it has since been assumed, that with our love of mimicry but also with our slovenly language habits, we coined the name 'the Moslem' for the upstairs sitting-room which came into its own on Sundays, high days and holidays.

Any small group, the members of which are held firmly together by bonds of love, duty, affection, or alienation from those without – street corner gangs, central bankers, mess mates, mining butties or families – has its own private and distinctive totems, ceremonies, signs, taboos and more particularly, language. We never showed any interest in the private code made up by my father and Great-uncle Morton. We had our own whistles for intimate communication. They were made up by my brothers and their friends and covered most of the normal daily communication of people who can anticipate fairly accurately the pattern of one another's lives. Their whistling did not need to be as sophisticated as that exchanged between Panamanian bootblacks, nor to carry as far as the whistling of shepherds in the Balearic Islands, but it was a highly developed code of signals nevertheless.

In addition to this we had our own terminology, intimate and exclusive. With a biblical boom: 'trump' for fart, 'Fair arrered' for tired, 'sloken for dee-ad' for thirsty; 'bug-rake' for comb; 'fessie' for lavatory; and, on the index of absolutely forbidden words, 'bumscrape' to describe a delicious, patent yeast extract for spreading on toast, and, somewhat mysteriously, 'con' to identify anyone bumptious of manner. These are some of the words and phrases which, like 'the Moslem' still remain in use.

In spite of an excessive amount of furniture and bric-à-brac, the Moslem remained spacious and elegant, if not particularly inviting. Although it faced west and had long, sash windows through which the light of summer streamed, the overwhelming effect was sombre. The room was stuffed with armchairs and sofas filled with tasselled cushions and defended by antimacassars of intricately crocheted Maltese lace. It was dominated by my mother's German piano, and there seemed little room to manoeuvre. The walls were hung with my mother's watercolours, light, romantic, elegant even, but weighted down by dull, heavy oak frames as if they were determined to deny the beauty of what they imprisoned. Hung almost absentmindedly as if awaiting someone to come in and use them were a Zulu knobkerrie, finely carved boomerangs and throwing sticks, a Lincolnshire Yeomanry sabre, a German cavalry helmet, a sola topee and a soldier uncle's dress sword. Over the highest of several bookcases was a luridly coloured photograph of Great-uncle Morton's steam yacht with its villanous-looking Turkish crew clearly visible.

The floor was covered by a large number of oriental rugs, kept reverse side up except when best company was expected, with small tables placed strategically to cover the balder spots. With the exception of one, these tables were crowded with photographs of a ghostly regiment of cousins, looking sternly at the camera but somehow helplessly vulnerable, about to be sucked all unknowing into the mud of Flanders fields. The

. . . stuffed with armchairs and sofas

table that alone was kept clear was a high, walnut one inlaid with ivory on which my brothers taught me draughts, or checkers; my father chess; my Great-uncle Alfred backgammon; and the prince the fast and furious game of halma that he had brought back from Baghdad. When we played halma he would frighten me with the ferocity of his attack, as if he was seeking evidence of a tensile mental strength and already testing the sinews of manhood in someone who was still only half-whelped: *mal lêché*, as he put it when he despaired of me.

Amidst all this clutter and accumulation, the Moslem had a centre of focus: the fireplace. Beneath a massive looking-glass, encased in white, grey-veined marble and green and black tiles, with an outer barbican of brass fire irons, fender and coal scuttles, there blazed at all seasons of the year, save on the hottest summer days, a high-banked coal fire. Its hearth was Mrs Belton's delight to wash and blacklead. At harvest time she would decorate it with corn dollies made by our farming relatives from the gleanings. As a result of this ancient propitiation to pagan gods to ensure fertility, the fireplace assumed something of the aura of a family shrine. It certainly served as a sanctuary for, in this spacious and generous but very busy household, it was only there that each of us was entitled to sit and dream.

We were strict Sabbatarians in practice but not in faith. Neither because Jesus rose on the third day nor because on the seventh God rested from his labours did we observe Sunday as a day of quiet and no work; but, simply because Saturday was Market Day and the demanding culmination of a week of increasing frenetic commercial activity from sunrise until – even in those northern latitudes of summer – sundown. By Sunday morning a strange, almost uncanny quiet reigned over a yard which only the evening before had been crowded with drays, cars and carts. The stillness remained undisturbed until abruptly rocked from its meditations by the peals from the church tower announcing the approach of matins. Sabbath observance was little more and nothing less than the need for a respite from unrelenting, daily demands.

None of us was pressed to go to church or chapel, Sunday

school or any similar gathering. Quaker meeting was two hours away and attended only monthly as it was something of an expedition to get there on time. So we were left to our own devices except on fine Sundays when we all clambered into the car clutching buckets, spades, kites and small sailing boats, preceded by wicker hampers of food, pop, towels and changes of clothing securely wedged into the boot with tartan travelling rugs and camping stools. But there would be no seaside journey to the sands at Sutton or the dunes at Huttoft if Brown or Frank had forgotten to fill up with petrol or to check the oil on the day before.

On Sundays the line was finely but clearly drawn. No laundry was done. In any case Mrs Blades, our washerwoman, arrived at eight o'clock on Monday, already hot and perspiring, to plunge into the washhouse in whose copper, however, we had put into soak on Sunday the workmen's heavy clothes and aprons. But they were not to be stirred with the dolly: only soaked. The copper fire could be laid, but not lit. When these mores were critically examined by her children – with a view to overturning them – my mother would respond by telling us that in *her* mother's day, amongst many severities now happily discontinued, the piano was locked on Saturday night and the harmonium unlocked. Fortunately for us all, this sanctimonious horror had, as my mother put it, run out of puff around the time of Queen Victoria's diamond jubilee (possibly due to an assault on it by wicked Uncle Jack) and had to be put down. She would add darkly that we should consider ourselves lucky. Thus as a would-be revolutionary I learned my first lesson: revolts do not erupt from starvelings arising from their slumbers, but from those of us who have never had it so good. But mother knew that a mention of the piano would quell any incipient revolt over Sunday in the Moslem.

For it was the piano which formed the hub of our little universe on a Sunday morning. Fresh from his bath my father would begin, well in advance of the church bells, to play his favourite hymns. The prince would join him after exchanging his frogged dressing gown for a tweed suit, his light tenor voice mingling with my father's husky baritone. My mother would come in later, being delayed by supervising the day's domestic arrangements and, should the summer be cold or rainy, as a final task, pinning into my clean Sunday shirt the new square of Thermogene.

Joining the men she would replace my father at the piano. His favourites were played and sung first: 'Just a song at Twilight' was no longer followed by 'Lead, Kindly Light' as it had been determined that Newman had already 'gone over to Rome' by the time he wrote the poem. Sacred songs were followed by favourites from *The Merry Widow*. Being Sunday there were no music hall ditties permitted, although my mother relented with Sir Harry Lauder's 'Coming Through The Rye'. No barrack-room ballads either, except the lovely one from the Boer War:

> Farewell my Bluebell, farewell to you.
> One long, last look into your eyes so blue.
> By camp fires gleaming, through shot and shell
> I shall be dreaming of my own Bluebell.

By this time the church bells were ringing, calling for an interval during which flutes were assembled and tuned. At this point Frank, now grown up, joined the group with his piccolo. The rest of us stayed next door in the nursery, or went down to the washhouse to clean our boots – one permitted Sunday task. It might be seen as a triumph of cleanliness over Godliness.

The church bells silent, and the only sounds being the hurried clatter of heels of those who were late for church and the gurgle of the river immediately below the bridge, the group thus strengthened would play Schubert and Schumann *lieder* – with the prince offering a translation where needed. This was the high point of the morning. From then on all was downhill. Frank gave a virtuoso rendering of the Overture to *William Tell*. This was followed by a somewhat ragged playing of Schubert's *Marche Militaire* with the prince joining in with a tin whistle. And, as a special treat for the prince, my father would sit at the piano and thump out and sing the musical hall song which was the source of the phrase 'jingoism'. And so it

... the prince joining in with a tin whistle

might have been because it was roared out in the London music halls in 1878, when Disraeli had conjured up the Russian xenophobia which then lay so close to the surface of the Londoner:

We don't want to fight
But by Jingo if we do
We've got the men we've got the ships
We've got the money too.

We've fought the bear before
And we have provisions more
For the Russians shall not have
Constantino-o-o-ple.

This the prince loved. But by then my mother, who would have disapproved, would have left to see what state her household was in and how fared the preparations for the stupendous Sunday luncheon. The dining table had already been covered with the heavy, white damask cloths, the starching of which delighted the heart of Mrs Blades. Throughout the morning it was unlaid, devoid of glass, silver or china, like an altar after Maundy Thursday awaiting the sacrificial lamb.

While we were free to enter the Moslem whenever we chose, by unspoken consent it was left as the private preserve on Sunday morning of the grown-ups. The desert of the afternoon stretched ahead when grown-ups dozed in their rooms and we were encouraged to go for improving walks along the waterside. Harold, however, joined the Methodist Young Men's Brotherhood – probably in order to captain the football team. The Brotherhood was composed for the most part of his whistling confrères and had as its motto the ominous 'Remember now thy Creator, in the days of thy youth'. Ominous, for the phrase left something dangling. What was it? 'While the evil days come not, nor the years draw nigh, when thou shalt say, I have no pleasure in them. . . . Or ever the silver cord be loosed, or the golden bowl be broken. . . . Vanity of vanities, saith the preacher; all is vanity.' Sunday afternoon, therefore, was a treeless plain unrelieved, I would imagine, in Harold's case by the lugubriousness of the Brotherhood. But the plains once traversed led to the high hills in which all our creative talents were unleashed, for the evenings in the Moslem belonged solely and exclusively to the prince and ourselves.

On Sunday evenings the Sunday Book under the direction of the prince was opened by Frank. Alongside, a small mountain of corks, sealing wax, candle ends, cardboard boxes, cellophane bags, cotton reels, lavatory rolls, matches, margarine boxes, glue, scissors, rulers and wire from orange crates together with the week's accumulation of newspaper had all been gathered in anticipation.

First we made a start on the weekly drawing. This was a Russian sleigh drawn by five horses, the sleigh from the prince's own childhood, and the five of us were harnessed to it.

The prince drew the sleigh – head on – leaving the outline of five horses in the traces. Carefully, throughout the evening, each of us would paint or crayon in one horse with a head that resembled his own: a fine way to keep the unoccupied busy. At the end of the evening the prince would draw in himself as the driver complete with furs, cigar and cough medicine bottle, sometimes pursued by bears.

Then we would each assume a separate task. Jane almost always made a nest of drawers from six England's Glory matchboxes glued together, covered in wallpaper fragments with mother-of-pearl buttons sewn on the drawers for handles. If she exhausted the supply of empty matchboxes, she contented herself with a row of clothes-peg dolls. Harold took a lavatory roll and with a knife cut sections and folded them outwards in the shape of wings and horns. These he coloured lavishly to make a frightening totem pole. Muriel, who was often restless possibly because of her lameness, fashioned huge paper propellers in different stripes of colour which she festooned with pins wherever there was a current of air – from the fireplace or the windows. I, wanting a tank to knock down my lead soldiers, took a used cotton reel, and with the prince's help notched the rim, took some candle grease and warmed it in my palm and plugged it round a match to which was attached the elastic taken earlier in the day from a crate of empty stout bottles. (One brand, possibly Mackeson's, was sold with a fancy paper cover over the screw top and this was secured by a small but strong elastic band. A stealthy trip up the inn yard and a quick rummage through the empties, stacked by the landlady from the bacchanal of Saturday night, yielded a handsome harvest of rubber bands.) The wax plugged one end of the hole in the cotton reel, the elastic was threaded through and attached to a kitchen match. Wound up, the match would propel the tank which would then rumble forward leaving a path of devastation in its wake. As the power drive was on one end of the machine only, the tank ran round in circles. Thus a kind of poetic justice was meted out, my own forces suffering a similar fate to that of the enemy.

Frank's primary task was to make meticulous scale drawings

... leaving a path of devastation

of all that was undertaken. Aware of an ability that had apparently passed our parents' notice and which we dismissed as finickiness, the prince recognized a delight in precision and engineering neatness which, when coupled to an artistic flair, resulted in some remarkably elegant work. Frank's obsessiveness had found its rightful place. Like Leonardo's notebooks, the Sunday Book recorded not only our experiments, but also our aspirations.

Looking through it now it seemed that, in later years as we grew older, we turned to scientific experiment with Frank the principal laboratory assistant. First came our equipment. This included balances, in the making of which we all played a part. I cut a cork; Muriel pushed a knitting needle through it; Jane found two tumblers; and Harold sank two nails, one at each end to balance the cork on the inverted glasses. Frank tied the delicate cottons on which the pans swung on each end of the knitting needle. Harold foraged for rice in the warehouse as we needed a few grains to serve as units of measure. Then we were ready to weigh feathers, hairs, pins and needles and, when the prince went out for a swig of cough medicine, nose pickings.

Cotton reels and coat hangers were strung up across the Moslem to form pulleys, blocks and cranes of enormous complexity. Frank carefully recorded how many feet of line had to be taken in to move one foot of weight on the hook with each additional pulley. Galileo's pendulum made with different-sized apples on strings of different lengths confounded our sense of what was commonsense.

A whole section shows us advancing on the bathroom with carefully wrought water wheels of darning needles for shafts, corks and cut-up postcards for vanes; speedboats of cardboard with camphor ball engines; galleons made with corks with farthing keels, matchstick masts and paper sails; and channel buoys made of corks and silver paper. I remember how we grunted and pushed at one another for space in the bathtub for our engines and devices.

The distances between a pivot and the weight required to balance a seesaw were carefully measured with pennies on a ruler over an up-ended matchbox. On another occasion we experimented with heating air and alarmed Kathleen by squeezing a hard-boiled egg into a milk bottle and then out again. Every bedroom had its own private weather vane of corks and matches. Frank had an addition for measuring air pressure with an inverted jam jar (little knowing that a distant forebear was the inventor of the rain-gauge). Finally, the greatest excitement of all was the creation of the Bernoulli effect from blowing on a piece of paper to make wings for paper aeroplanes that flew from attic windows. It was all a very heady business with the prince leading us like the Pied Piper. Had it not been for Frank measuring and recording, we might all have danced our way up a Koppelberg Hill of our own making and into the mountainside.

Sunday in the Moslem ended with cocoa and biscuits, the prince completing the sleigh drawing, putting in his own face with fearsome features above the driver's collar and below the cossack hat. All was copied in the Sunday Book with loving and meticulous care by Frank. It was closed and put away. I was then led off to bed. On Sundays in summer the bitter bile of resentment gagged in my throat. For it was still a bright day outside and my elder brothers and sisters stayed on in the Moslem for additional delights from which I was excluded. But that was the price you paid for being the youngest in the family. . . .

I have to go to bed and see
The birds still hopping in the tree,
Or hear the grown-up people's feet
Still going past me in the street.

NINE

'What Are They Doing To Our Lottie?'

... Muriel continued her bombardment

W hen, in the midst of a most solemn religious service, Muriel created mayhem bordering on riot, causing substantial damage to chapel property, aided and abetted by Harold (nature's own *agent provocateur*), supported to a lesser extent by Frank and Jane, I was, alas, too young to be present. It was always an invigorating sight to see Muriel in full flight.

I suspect that she had always been wilful and strong-headed. Her being badly thrown from a pony when still very young resulted in prolonged suffering, a long convalescence and permanent injury to her right leg. Sufficiently severe was the damage that the surgeons who attended her doubted whether she would ever walk again.

Their calculations could hardly have been expected to take fully into account a native resilience that became transmuted into a grim determination. Once she was up and about, my parents prudently purchased a Raleigh bicycle for her from Nunkie Brown. From then onwards there was no holding her. With her crippled leg swathed in bandages and stuck out at an alarming angle she peddled furiously on one foot and careered around the town and, in due course, the countryside. Soon she was swinging a tennis racquet and, not long afterwards, was once again seen cantering along the pine-scented rides in the forest at Woodhall. Later, after some Manichean heart-searching, our parents consented to her joining the local dancing class.

Much of my childhood was spent in witnessing Muriel overcoming adversity. It invested in me a much-needed stoicism when personal handicap and suffering made their periodic appearance. And if Muriel seemed to me, as I grew older, to lack charity, it was a small price paid for not being crippled physically or, for that matter, emotionally.

Lottie, who inadvertently caused the disturbance in the Baptist chapel, by the time I knew her was the highly respected wife of the Louth church clock-winder and town lamp-lighter. A figure of romance as he strolled at dusk through the streets with his long pole igniting the gas lamps, we used to tag along with him when, in winter, we went to tea with Lottie. Short in

... pedalled furiously on one foot

stature, when she was working in my mother's household a soap box was provided for her to stand on in the scullery. Thus mounted, she sang while washing the dishes hymns highly evangelical in content.

My father endeared himself to her for ever one Sunday when one of our distant archdeacon relatives who was staying with us made at luncheon some slighting reference to Lottie's denomination. He frequented circles where, apparently one spoke at table as if the servants were stone deaf. My father defused the situation with a typical response: 'Of course, Baptists are awful; but at least their sect was founded by John the Baptist. Who founded yours? Oh, that syphilitic madman, Henry VIII. Unless. . . .' And at this point he waved the carving knife in the general direction of his guest, not so much as to threaten but to illustrate the point. 'Unless,' he repeated, 'you are one of those who are indulging in a flirtation with the Scarlet Woman of Rome.' Mrs Blades had, indeed, remarked earlier that the archdeacon's clerical collars were somewhat narrower than before. Of this she approved, not being bemused by doctrinal conflicts, for the collars needed less starching on wash day.

Although I missed out on Lottie's songs of praise, I did enjoy those of Mrs Belton. They, unlike Lottie's, were positively sepulchral, usually written by that prolific hymnalist Isaac Watts. Washing up was not Mrs Belton's demesne, but she loved to clear the ashes, blacklead the grates and lay the fires. When the kindling was well lit in the coals she would take a soapy floor-cloth and wash the surrounding tiles, making the fire hiss delightfully as she caught the edge of the cinders with the damp cloth. The rituals of cleaning and preparing a grate to receive the new day's fire is most satisfying, as I can attest. It was welcomed with a hymn by Mrs Belton. Her thin Gyrwie voice would lament:

> Days and hours are quickly fly-ing
> Blends the living with the de-ad;
> Soon now you and I'll be ly-ing
> Cold within our narrow be-ad
> > Narrow be-ad.

This evoked shades of Andrew Marvell:

> The grave's a fine and private place,
> But none I think do there embrace.

The hymn that most thrilled me, recalling startling horrors from Foxe's *Book of Martyrs* was William Cowper's:

> There is a fountain filled with ber-lood,
> Drawn from I-mmanuel's veins;
> And sinners plunged be-neath the fer-lood,
> Lose all their guilty stains.
> And sinners plunged beneath the fer-lood
> Lose all their guilty stains.

The Beltons bordered on being Particular and Peculiar People and, on a weekday night, would repair to a little tin Bethel where they would be treated to a hell-fire sermon and extensive, extemporized prayer, and sing more Isaac Watts.

They took me there once. A wise providence intervened when a summer storm broke over our heads. The corrugated iron roof so resounded with the bouncing hail that our devotions were first deafened and then abandoned.

The kindling laid by Mrs Belton was chopped by her husband. Badly gassed towards the end of the Great War, he would spend much of the day standing very still, with his hand leaning on something for support while his poor lungs fought for air before he could lift a hatchet, pick up a rake or fork some earth into his wheelbarrow. He never complained and was treated with honour. Their son, Eric, was my hero. It was he who, after a stint in the Royal Air Force when I was about nine, had given me his walking-out swagger stick with the silver knob on top. When he came back to civilian life he joined our bakery as a roundsman and sometimes helped in the bakehouse. I used to dog his footsteps, getting in his way until, for the sake of peace, he would stop what he was doing and give me his attention. He taught me to ride Muriel's bicycle before my legs were long enough for me to sit on the saddle, and sometimes, in his lunch hour, would let me spar with him. Behind the Belton's cottage under a huge elm tree we would don the mitts, I swinging haymakers at him while he danced away, dotting me one here and there until I lay exhausted on the grass.

The year the missionary came to stay Eric made for me what became my proudest possession. My wicked Uncle Jack had sent in his Christmas parcel from Calgary a full Indian headdress with a useless toy tomahawk. I showed this to Eric who, without a word, led me to a willow tree on the river bank and quickly cut a stout four-foot-long branch and trimmed and notched it at both ends. He bent it into a bow with a piece of thin sash cord we found in the bottom warehouse and slung it over my shoulder. Searching among the boxes his father used for firewood, he took several short lengths and split and notched them at one end. Then he sent me off to find some stiff paper for the feathering while he cut some short bits of thin elder branch. He pushed the shaft of each arrow into the soft pith of the elder, poking it out the other end until the arrow

...flighted it with unerring accuracy

head was firmly embedded in the cut piece. Then he looked around for a target and, spotting Nunkie's Dragon across the river, took the bow from me, fitted an arrow and flighted it with unerring accuracy. It hit the mouthpiece of the exhaust pipe with a resounding clang. Eric handed me the bow and the bundle of arrows and went home to his tea.

By the time the lapsed missionary of the Society for the Propagation of the Gospel among the Jews had arrived, I had lost many arrows and, two broken windows later, become a passable bowman. The missionary pointed out that the Israelite archer always had five arrows to his quiver, so five arrows I had at a time on my forays. I remember the number because my father once annoyed a childless aunt by loftily informing her that on marriage he had always intended 'to have his quiverful'. I was the fifth, and last, child to be born.

My father had a certain reputation for being 'a bit of a slave-driver'. But he was also fiercely protective of those in his employ. Not only from the outside world, such as when the archdeacon laughed at Lottie or when someone sneered at Tommy, the yardman, for being illiterate, but also when we as a family got out of hand. We were expected to observe a personal rectitude towards others. The one person we were allowed to chuckle about, however, was 'Dripping-tin' Sowden, Great-uncle Alf Dunham's waggoner.

His was another example of our curious habit of mispronouncing names. Not until after Sowden's death did I learn that his name was Snowden, not Sowden. He was a fine waggoner and, in the subsequent era of the combustion engine, his descendants became excellent drivers. Sowden's wife was excessively houseproud. Coming in for his midday meal with boots encrusted with mud and manure. Sowden would be required to sit at table with his feet in an old roasting pan, the kind known in Lincolnshire as a 'dripping-tin' – for it was in such a piece of ironmongery that on a Sunday the Yorkshire pudding was cooked as the joint dripped on it from above. Four generations later, origin forgotten, the cognomen is still used to distinguish Sowden's family from others of the same name who lived in our Lindsey district. The only time I have found anything similar was in a family of trawlermen whose remote ancestor of lusty and ungovernable appetites, in dire need on a prolonged expedition to the White Sea, had had sexual relations with a skate. Succeeding generations of his descendants continued to be identified as 'Skatey'.

None of us would ever have thought to mangle the Beltons' name, so close were they to us, and the closest was Kathleen. She came to us when I was three and she seventeen. In the beginning I remember little about her except the warmth of her smile, and her legs forever encased in black woollen stockings. In the two years before the gigantic bath was installed in a new bathroom off the 'boys' room' I was bathed in a copper tub in front of the fire. I made a habit of lying on my back watching the firelight dance on the ceiling so that Kathleen would have to step over me as she brought in cans of hot water. Then I would gaze entranced with the way her black-stockinged legs disappeared into layers of white, starched undergarments. Here was mystery indeed: further dreaming of which was promptly dispelled in the bath by a rapid and coruscating application of a loofah.

... disappeared into layers
of white starched
undergarments

That Kathleen was almost one of the family, participating in our noisy games as well as caring for her young charges, is borne out by her appearance in most of our family snapshots. She is seen in the canoe with Muriel, playing badminton with Jane, accompanying my mother on outings and enjoying herself with Frank and Harold at the August Gala. Her standing in the family must also have been very secure, for it was she who stalwartly withstood my father's outrage when Muriel came back from a shopping expedition to Lincoln with a pair of high-heeled crocodile-skin shoes. He was horrified at what he regarded as a display of ostentation and a departure from his principles of plain living. Kathleen managed to deflect his anger from Muriel; but he was so incensed that he forgot to turn off the spigot of a drum of molasses which he had tilted to drain overnight in an outhouse – the one in which the clean bread baskets were kept. In the morning he found a veritable lake of sticky, black treacle oozing out into the yard. The following Sunday at Quaker Meeting he spoke of the dangers that lie in wait for the overbearing and intolerant.

As might be expected, Kathleen came in for her share of family teasing. She was often reminded of the occasion when, in my mother's absence, she asked my father where to take me in my perambulator for the afternoon. He, perhaps with his mind on his Friday meeting with the Reverend Isaacs, suggested that she take me to see Morton Bey. Kathleen, not having much sense of geography but a fine bump of location, put me in the push chair and headed eastwards towards the sea. She assumed that if she took the road to the coast over Dunham Hills through Partney, she would eventually reach 'Morton Bay'. Uncle Morton Bey, of course, lived two miles away at Moda House on Thimbleby Top. Fortunately Kathleen and I were rescued by Great-uncle Tommy Dunham in his 1907 De Dion Bouton motor as he came upon her trudging in the heat up his brother's hills. He brought us both home in triumph with his parrot in its cage dangling dangerously over the exhaust (from the fumes of which, several years later, it expired). It was just as well we were discovered as the coast was twenty-one miles away and there is no Morton Bay.

Uncle Tommy was an 'ickeny' Dunham who, of all great-grandfather's seven sons, was the only one not to become a farmer, corn merchant or wool buyer. Electing to devote his life to hunting, shooting and fishing, he needed to supplement his private income. Being a Dunham, he also liked to keep a close eye on his money. Through a family connexion, he killed both birds by becoming a manager in the Capital and Counties Bank. The branches where he served were small and obscure, carefully chosen for their proximity to his sporting interests, and requiring his presence only perfunctorily. In retirement by the time I knew him, he lived in bachelor comfort at Ashby Puerorum. Always something of a recluse, he had his De Dion which brought him to market, the parrot which provided him with the only companionship he needed and a retired game-keeper who looked after him.

Acknowledged but avoided by his brothers, Tommy adored my mother. He was friendly with the prince and they went shooting together. Uncle Tommy, though, had curious culinary preferences. Once he ate on Easter Sunday a pheasant he had shot the previous Boxing Day. It barely needed cooking. Another time he left a hare hanging too long in the larder; after several weeks it became so ripe even the game-keeper protested and buried it. The next day Tommy asked to have his hare for dinner. Learning what had happened he ordered the hare exhumed – and ate it with great relish and a liberal helping of redcurrant jelly. It was fortunate that it was Uncle Tommy who rescued us, for with him no explanation of the contretemps was necessary. He would never have dreamed of asking.

... came back from a shopping expedition to Lincoln

Soon after I went to boarding school Kathleen married a postman and went to live in Hull. Unhappily, we saw her only rarely after that, as she could not often visit her parents who remained in Horncastle. If her earliest memory of me was my eating a boiled egg, my earliest memory was of the Stanton Hill Colliery Band who came to our town during the miners' strike of 1927. It was the only time I saw together in our yard everyone mentioned in this chapter.

Collieries along with heavy industry belonged to the smoky lands beyond the Trent – the haze of which we could see rising far to the west from the top of the Lincolnshire Edge. Miners were part of another world, and their entry into ours was entirely fortuitous. Trade and industry had suffered badly after the Great War and in 1926 miners were faced with a cut in their already meagre wages. Their refusal to accept this led to the General Strike and a prolonged and embittered continuation by the miners alone, after those in other trades who had employment had long since returned to work. In search of support, colliery brass and silver bands from all over the country marched towards London to demonstrate, playing for their keep along the way and in the hope of boosting the diminishing welfare funds in their distant pit villages.

One hot July afternoon in 1927 – I must have been about four years old at the time – Jane and I were playing in the upstairs sitting-room. It was one of those rare, still, summer days. The light danced on the water below the open windows and threw a flickering pattern on the walls and ceiling. The air was heavy and no sound came from the street, empty in the hot afternoon. We played rather listlessly, almost as if waiting for something more interesting to happen.

Suddenly we heard, but only very faintly in the distance, a band playing. The sound became louder, and then louder as the band approached down West Street. We rushed to the window and scrambled up on the window seat just in time to see it – cornets, trombones, tubas and trumpets flashing in the sunlight as the band swung round the corner by the Fighting Cocks and up Bridge Street, the bandsmen in parade step, immaculate in blue uniforms with silver piping. When they reached our bridge they stopped playing, put down their instruments and grounded their packs. It must have been a Wednesday, the half-day closing, as all the shops were shut. The bandsmen had marched the twenty-one miles from Lincoln across the wolds and through the villages, carrying their kit and lugging their instruments past closed shops with drawn blinds. No hope of refreshment there. But although our shop too was closed, my father was in the yard, and seeing their plight he ran out and ushered them into the garden. It transpired that they were the Stanton Hill Silver Prize Colliery Band which we listened to from time to time on our newly acquired His Master's Voice gramophone. They thought they had been marching towards London from their pit villages in Derbyshire, but in some mysterious way when they reached Lincoln they had turned east instead of south.

The response to their needs was immediate. What reservoirs of goodwill were drawn on, unpaid debts liquidated and consciences pricked! Muriel, Kathleen and Jane got going on the refreshments. Frank and Harold were despatched to get mattresses and an old field kitchen from the drill hall. People came with brooms to help sweep the warehouses still sweet from the wool clip. Mrs Blades supervised the moving of an old copper under a lean-to. Wonder of wonders, Great-uncle Alfred appeared with three hams. His brother Arthur sent a waggon of clean straw and a flitch of bacon. Tommy the yardman polished boots and Hogg the cobbler came with his bench to repair them. A fruiterer, who in 1914 as an impoverished Belgian refugee had been set up with a market stall by my mother, presented his entire day's stock of vegetables and fruit. Other victuals came from the granary or the warehouses. Uncle Tommy and his gamekeeper arrived with rabbits. Nunkie Brown unexpectedly lent a canteen of cutlery and a pantry-full of dishes. The gunsmith's Russian wife came to help Mrs Blades.

My brothers took the bandsmen to bathe in the river. Their shirts were stuffed in the copper. (Later it would be used to boil their dinner). Trestles were put up in the yard, mattresses laid in the warehouse, and order was restored by the Beltons.

While the colliers' clothes were being washed they sat in jackets and trousers and were regaled with a great meal of ham and pork and rabbit stew. In the evening Jane and I crept out to peer at the sleeping men. They were not people as I knew them. Thin, emaciated and grey-faced, their hands were scarred and their features etched with years of coal dust. In their sleep they coughed in short, dry spasms, like Belton having one of his 'turns'.

By Saturday market day they had settled into a quiet routine of bathing, eating and sleeping. Instruments were polished, uniforms brushed and letters written home. A small group joined Muriel and Harold playing tennis. They were quietly intent, and spoke in accents difficult for us to follow. That evening, though, the market stalls dismantled, not a breath of wind stirring, the traffic stilled and even the rooks silent, we heard from the garden the strains of 'Abide with Me'. There, in full regalia, the bass drummer in his leopardskin and the bandmaster wearing his 'Pip, Squeak and Wilfred' war decorations, they played for my father. Before long, first the bridge, then both banks of the river were crowded. Our yard and those of our neighbours became jammed. Family, relatives, friends and maids filled our windows like a Stanley Spencer painting. We were all there, Dunhams, Pouchers, Townleys, townsfolk, countryfolk, itinerant costers standing silent, knowing that we had received a great gift.

The coming of the miners' band to Horncastle is my earliest recollection. Had I been a year or so older I would probably have joined those invited to Lottie's baptism. Knowing that my mother found religious rites distasteful and that my father, being a Quaker, did not countenance ritual of any kind, Lottie asked if my brothers and sisters could be present as her guests when she was baptized. But she had given only some general indication of her 'sins being washed away' at the ceremony.

Thus, not knowing quite what to expect, Frank, Muriel, Harold and Jane went with Lottie to Cagthorpe at the end of the town where stood a modest but elegantly proportioned Georgian building. It now houses the Salvation Army, but in those days it was the Baptist Chapel. Crowded into a gallery, issued with hymn books and told by an usher to keep quiet, they settled down to observe the proceedings. Muriel, to protect her bandaged leg, sat at the far end in the front row. With their heads peering through the rail they watched diminutive Lottie in her shift appear before a huge, bearded man. The congregation sang with easy familiarity 'We Shall Gather At the River'. The floorboards were taken up revealing a pool of water. At the request of the preacher Lottie renounced the Devil and all his works. (This made Muriel restless.) Then the congregation sang 'Tho' Your Sins be as Scarlet . . .', and the preacher jumped into the pool. Lottie followed him into the water. The congregation bellowed 'Halleluiah!', and Lottie was grabbed from behind and thoroughly dunked.

'What are they doing to our Lottie?' came the now memorable words from Muriel who, seeing no one rushing to the little woman's rescue, punctuated her screams of alarm by throwing her and Jane's hymn books at the preacher. Lottie, surfaced, choking. Hearing the rumpus she signalled that all was well, but imprisoned in the front row of a crowded gallery Muriel interpreted this as a mute appeal for help. So, amply supplied from behind with more hymn books by Harold, Muriel continued her bombardment accompanied by supporting shouts from the other children. The usher tried in vain to intervene. But ushers are there to provide an odour of sanctity, not to be chuckers-out of four obstreperous children. It is not clear how the day ended, whether Lottie had time to dry out and change from her damp shift in order to bring the children home, but I do know that Lottie's Jordan was my family's Rubicon. Never again would any of them attend any church ritual other than weddings and funerals, and then only those of the simplest kind.

This show of spirits on Muriel's part was the first of many outbursts that, as we grew older, took the form of a very natural rebellion against parental authority. Being the youngest by several years, I found dissension in the family both confusing and alarming. This reached its climax a few years later over the tragedy of Mrs Winters.

... *reading St. Paul's first letter to the Corinthians*

*T*hey hanged Mrs Winters at eight o'clock on a summer morning in 1931. A light drizzle was falling. As the clock above Lincoln prison gates struck the hour, a low moan came up from the prison inmates joined by a frenzied banging of tin cups and mess plates on the pipes, bars and anything else that reverberated in the gaol. Outside, my father stood bareheaded reading St Paul's First Letter to the Corinthians. He was startled momentarily by the prince dropping to his knees and crossing himself. So was Mrs van der Elst, who, at the same moment, stepped out from under the umbrella held by her chauffeur and hoisted a placard announcing the view that hanging, not the murderer, should be condemned. It was a role she played at every execution in the country: a rich, solitary, persistent opponent of capital punishment throughout her life.

The quartet stood separately from the small crowd of locals who at all times and places turn out for an execution. They remained until the chief warden came out through the Judas Gate set in the prison's great doors and pinned up a notice certifying execution and confirming death. The warden having surveyed his handiwork gazed stolidly at the onlookers for a moment and then returned to the gaol. As the gate banged shut, almost as if the sound had served as a signal, the hysterical clatter of pans stopped and the moaning died away. Mrs van der Elst handed the placard back to her chauffeur, exchanging it for her umbrella and immediately invited my father and the prince to breakfast at the White Hart.

Whether as a by-product of the malt kilns or from some other source, my father had marketed a malted bran which, when sprinkled over Force – the only processed cereal available in the twenties and early thirties in England – or over the more familiar porridge, added bulk to breakfast. This must have been around 1930, for the prince returning from Nuristan had brought back some Hatha Yoga techniques and new ideas on diet. He pressed both on my father who became diligent in learning and practising Yoga, but the new diet was diverted to swelling his bank balance rather than to reducing his waistline.

Father's first meeting with Mrs Winters was when she called

to thank him for, as she put it, 'saving my life'. The bran had become her breakfast staple strengthening her 'nerves' and, as she subsequently imparted privately to my mother, kept her 'regular' in her daily visits to the outhouse.

Mrs Winters, while not frail, certainly did not have the robustness of the more prosperous farmers' wives. Like our sausages, they were shining, round, fat, bulging and seamless. They also glistened for, encased in creaking whalebone, they perspired freely at all seasons. My mother, much to the discomfiture of the rest of us, was always flinging up windows to freshen a room after they had left regardless of how wet or turbulent the weather.

It might have been my mother's hatred of obesity and her sensitive nose that endeared Mrs Winters to her. She was slight in build, delicate of face and feature, fastidious in dress, finicky in manner and always enveloped in a light, lavender fragrance. 'Without doubt', I heard mother telling Muriel, 'she must have been in service at one time.' My mother had an eye for these things and sure enough Uncle George of Asgarby Grange, who employed Winters as his waggoner, said that she had indeed been lady's maid at Langton Hall before she married Winters.

This piece of intelligence excited my father who knew that Doctor Johnson had had as a close friend Bennet Langton, whose family owned the Hall and the surrounding lands. Doctor Johnson, however, had been particularly fascinated by Bennet's brother Peregrine, who lived over the wold at Partney in a neat little house with a paddock and a few acres. Looked after by his sister and niece, Peregrine lived comfortably, if not ostentatiously, with two maids, two liveried manservants, three horses and a post chaise – all on £200 a year. He entertained frequently and never had less than three or four different dishes at table. Doctor Johnson, to whose few friends he remained devoted, was so amazed at Peregrine's 'piety and oeconomy' that he contemplated emulating the rural life. Fortunately, for those who would have been his neighbours, he did not.

'Did you not know of Dr Johnson over at Langton?' my father asked Mrs Winters, who a moment before had been describing her state of health. 'Oh, no, Sir,' she replied, 'we have no doctor up there. If we need anything we go to Mr MacEvoy the bone-setter.'

It was MacEvoy who was to prove unwittingly to be Mrs Winter's undoing. He was the local veterinary surgeon. In remote country districts, where most injuries were fractures, sprains or strains, the vet more often than not provided simple medical services and cheerfully plastered, drenched and poulticed man and beast indiscriminately, even using the same medicaments. That Mrs Winters did not share my father's literary erudition on this point caused considerable amusement. And much to Kathleen's relief, it replaced the story, too often told at table, of her taking me to see Morton Bey.

So Mrs Winters, whose life my father had saved, visited us two or three times a year, sometimes when her husband came to market and always when he brought the wool clip – which was clean and sweet-smelling – to the Dunham warehouses further down the river from ours. Our first encounter with Winters was also the last. A surly brute, he was drunk, dishevelled and truculent when he came to find his wife. He was kept waiting at the side door, which did not improve his temper. He began to pound the big dolphin door knocker on the solid Spanish black mahogany door, setting up a reverberation in the hall that made my brother Frank feel, as he put it at supper, like the porter in *Macbeth*.

'Comm'un, Missus,' Winters bawled, 'b'aint got all day.' And, as he helped a flustered Mrs Winters up onto the wagon, 'you an' yer stuck-up ways. It's a whippin' yer want, then?' With that, the team tugged the wagon over the gravel under the archway and out of the yard. Mrs Winters never called again. If she came to Horncastle at all she visited a cousin who had opened a drapery business across the bridge. Winters was sometimes seen in the market, usually three sheets in the wind and exceedingly quarrelsome.

It was on a summer picnic to Asgarby that my mother asked after Mrs Winters. Uncle George reported that she had appeared at MacEvoy's with a badly wrenched arm, a bruised cheek and lacerated back. MacEvoy had gone immediately to

. . . *a surly brute*

Winters and, in Uncle George's barn, threatened to thrash him if anything like that happened again. Winters was subdued if not exactly contrite, and MacEvoy bristling with rage had returned to treat Mrs Winters with tincture of arnica. When the next beating took place MacEvoy was away. Uncle George, as he said later, felt he could do little, for Winters was a good waggoner and besides, wife-beating was not uncommon particularly in the winter months. He added that it was a pity that the couple did not have any children.

Mrs Winters, however, took matters into her own hands. She left her husband and went to live with her cousin over the draper's shop, where she kept house for him and served downstairs at the millinery counter. The tragedy would never have happened had Mrs Winters stayed to be abused and brutalized. It was her lot and, who knows to what extent the oppressed invite the oppressor? But handling the dainty lace and silks of the millinery counter with the bruises healing and the wash-tub chilblains becoming a memory of winter, like Hardy's Jude gazing from afar at the spires of Oxford, she glimpsed a life that was by its very nature hers: only, like Jude, to have the vision shattered. Abruptly Winters arrived, struck her, terrorized the draper, and without waiting for her to collect her things, rode homeward with her in sullen and brooding silence.

When we heard that Winters had died suddenly we were rather relieved. Not because we had worried much about her, but we shared my mother's anxiety that my father might be tempted to indulge in some quixotry on Mrs Winters' behalf. Now we expected her to return to her cousin: in fact, marry him. In Lincolnshire marrying a cousin was so frequent an occurrence as to call for no comment. But Mrs Winters remained alone in the cottage. Uncle George was very decent about letting her stay on, for it was a tied cottage and he really needed it for the new waggoner and his family.

Then one day a dog belonging to a gamekeeper on a neighbouring estate died after rummaging in a rubbish heap. It was the one that lay beyond Mrs Winters' privy. The food scraps the dog had eaten, MacEvoy confirmed, contained rat bane. If a cat had died no one would have thought twice about it; but a dog was a different matter and the rural constable had to be informed. This set in motion a chain of events that were remorseless in their outcome. Winters' corpse was exhumed. An autopsy was ordered. The remains revealed enough arsenic to poison all the rats in the county. Mrs Winters was arrested, charged with murder and committed for trial at Lincoln Assizes.

My father only saw Mrs Winters once more. On the last day of her trial he drove her cousin, the draper, to Lincoln to lend him some support and comfort. In court she looked pitifully small in her widow's weeds, her eyes cast down. They were present when the scarlet-robed judge slowly and carefully placed the square of black silk on top of his bewigged head and said with his eyes never leaving hers: 'The sentence of the court upon you is that you be taken from this place to a lawful prison and thence to the place of execution, and that you be hanged by the neck until you are dead; and that your body be afterward buried within the precincts of the prison in which you shall have been confined before your execution. And may the Lord have mercy on your soul.'

The children of Horncastle lived with two reminders of the fate that awaited those guilty of capital crimes. Hangman's Corner stood on slightly raised ground by the Wong, or common pasture, which in my youth served as our playing fields. It was here that the town gibbet stood, until the reforms of 1825 reducing as they did capital crimes from 135 to a handful, made it redundant. The Corner was part of our lives, although not everyone rushed to retrieve a lost cricket ball from the thicket that was supposed to feed on the bones buried beneath.

Also, Horncastle had been the home of William Marwood, England's last public hangman. He had a little shop in St Mary's Yard, down which in later years we passed daily to school. When summoned to ply his gruesome trade he would retire to the loft above the cobbler's bench where he kept coils of hemp to make his own ropes. (It was customary in those days to make a new noose for each hanging.) At Horncastle he invented and in many subsequent executions perfected, the Marwood or Hangman's Knot that was swift and sure. My mother used to say that you could tell how many hangings were awaiting him when, in his billycock hat, high collar and thick, chapel-going suit he bumped his carpetbag of ropes over our bridge on his way to the station.

His last execution was a multiple hanging: four in a row. In 1882, due to the unfortunate involvement of Kitty O'Shea with Charles Parnell, the Irish patriot, William Gladstone, the then Prime Minister, found himself embroiled – quite innocently – in an episode that was sufficiently unsavoury to cause some cabinet resignations, including that of the chief secretary for Ireland. Gladstone appointed Lord Frederick Cavendish to replace him. The day after arriving in Dublin to take up his duties, the new chief secretary and his permanent under-secretary, T. H. Burke, were stabbed to death while walking in Phoenix Park. These murders effectively prevented any progress being made towards Home Rule for Ireland.

It took two years to bring the assassins to book. After their execution in Dublin, Marwood was tracked back from Ireland by members of the Sinn Fein. They followed him to Lincoln. In the station refreshment room, as he waited for the Horncastle local to pull in, Marwood collapsed and died, while at the next table those who sought vengeance sat watching quietly.

To hang a woman, though, seemed particularly barbaric. We talked amongst ourselves. Could Mrs Winters be saved? The prince asked whether by any chance she could be pregnant, for no one could kill the innocent and unborn. If she were, would not execution be postponed until the child was born? I not only told my schoolmates of this but enlarged upon it from what I considered to be my irrefutable sources. In *Acts*, Judas fell headlong to his death 'after which he burst asunder . . . and all his bowels gushed out.' That was why women were hanged in corsets; if they were pregnant their babies would otherwise leap out at the moment of impact – for as everyone knew, children were born through the belly button. I enjoyed a short-lived notoriety. It ended abruptly when a fellow urchin reminded me that I had previously told them that I had overheard my mother telling Kathleen that Mrs Winters never wore corsets. But I could claim to have some standing in the matter.

While disembowelling was not an everyday topic of conversation, I had the previous year learned from the prince that Colonel Francis Towneley had been hanged, drawn and quartered for the part he had played in the Jacobite Rebellion. His name was never mentioned by my family, not because of his treason but because he was a Catholic. A lawyer who lived a quiet and blameless life in Lancashire, his imagination became fired by the 1745 rebellion of Charles James Stewart. As the clans swarmed south across the border, Francis Towneley declared himself for the Bonnie Prince and raised at his own expense a troop of horse. He became an instant cavalry commander and in the battle of Prestonpans, near his home, put to rout the fearsome dragoons of Colonel Cope. It was the last battle ever to be fought on English soil and, for winning it on the wrong side, Towneley was executed at Tyburn and his head set on a pike above Temple Bar.

All this I knew because the prince had taken me to Towneley Hall near Burnley, by 1902 a museum managed by the local authority. There, for an extra sixpence, we were allowed to see the colonel's head pickled in a kind of outsize jam jar. I examined it carefully because Townleys – and Towneleys – were granted free admission to the Hall and the janitor prided himself on recognizing the unimpressive but unmistakable family features on visitors before they could claim free access. Thus the sixpence admission became a half-crown tip.

Lest this account should appear to lack feeling or to rejoice in the macabre, I can only state that the horror of having known, however fleetingly, the condemned woman was overlaid by one that was much greater, the distress of which has never been entirely erased. After the trial and while Mrs Winters sat in her cell awaiting execution, the annual Farmers' Ball took place. Next to the Hunt Ball it was the main social event in the district. Dancing in our family was not so much forbidden as dismissed, for in the puritan tradition it was

... and handed her the steel-nibbed pen

considered an invitation to promiscuousness. However, Muriel had managed to attend dancing and deportment classes, possibly conniving with the doctor in claiming them as therapy for her injured leg. Came the Farmer's Ball and Muriel demanded to be allowed to go. Thanks to the prince, she prevailed against parental disapproval and off she went on his arm. The prince, who looked resplendent in white tie and tails, wisely left her to her contemporaries for most of the evening, claiming her only for the Viennese waltzes, the Valeta and the Gay Gordons, which last his Scottish nurse had taught him so long ago in the Crimea.

The next day our Sunday in the Moslem was interrupted by the arrival of Mrs Winters' cousin, the draper. He had brought a petition for clemency addressed to the Home Secretary to be signed by all adult members of the family and such staff as were there on a Sunday. Everyone signed, except Tommy, the yardman, who was illiterate. He made a cross and this was authenticated by the draper, who had by then some practice in such matters.

Finally my father turned to Muriel and handed her the steel-nibbed pen for, sleeping late after the ball, she had only just come down. I recall the event vividly because I was shocked to see her in a dressing gown. No one, ever, was allowed downstairs in a state of undress: not even on the occasion when the house caught fire.

'No,' said Muriel, 'hanging is too good for her.' The prince smiled absentmindedly and said: 'At least you should finish the quotation, "hanging is too good for him, said Mr Cruelty." '

My father stared at her in disbelief. 'Please, Muriel, we are waiting. Will you sign?' he said. Muriel dropped the pen. 'No!' she shouted, 'an eye for an eye, a tooth for a tooth!'

My father's anger left me shaking for days after. At the time I crouched down behind the bureau and covered my ears. My father became choleric and incoherent with rage and humiliation at his daughter's defiance of his wishes. Clutching his flute in his left hand I thought he would strike her. Muriel was adamant. Up went her little pointed chin to defy the wrath to come.

'She killed her man!' she shouted as she swept from the room to remain upstairs for the rest of the day. Could she have been quick-stepping the previous night to the strains of 'Frankie and Johnny'? Hardly; the song had yet to be composed. But where else could Muriel have found so banal a phrase?

It was the prince who brought a truce, if not peace. Late in the evening he went to my sisters' room and, having reinforced himself with a quick nip of cough medicine, sat on Muriel's bed and told her how gracefully she had danced at the ball and how beautiful she had looked. Then his voice deepened. Eavesdropping, I heard him recite:

It is sweet to dance to violins
When love and life are fair
To dance to flutes, to dance to lutes

Is delicate and rare;
But it is not sweet with nimble feet
To dance upon the air.

Muriel wept. So did I: not for Mrs Winters about to dance upon the air, but for a family rent to foundations that until then had seemed unassailable. It was not that the authority of my father was challenged and challenged successfully; but that the deep, mutual unspoken awareness of values, views and tastes not shared by the world at large, and which gave the family its cohesion, when put to the test had threatened to crumble.

On Monday Kathleen handed my father's morning tea to Muriel. She took it to his room. The door closed and I could hear the murmur of their voices. Muriel's revolt was never again mentioned in the family.

. . . she took it
to his room

... his mouth bulging on one side with hobnails

*E*xploration without explanation is simply not enough, and if my quest for cosmic awareness continued to elude me I nevertheless did not falter in its pursuit. But I was very much alone in these matters. My brothers and sisters, although endlessly patient, were intent upon their own devices as well as those duties and obligations that our household imposed. From these I was exempt, being the Benjamin of the family.

Even if my father's mind had not turned elsewhere I doubt if he would have joined me in my enterprises. At that time his position on religious and related matters was very much like Martin Luther's: a compound of great negatives. But at the Rectory at Hemingby he found the serenity lacking at home. Here in the Reverend Isaac's book-lined study, with the long windows overlooking the garden and the churchyard, my father's levity and seriousness would be most elegantly mixed and appreciated, his puritan zeal tempered by a gentler reasonableness. My mother, commanding as she did an extensive and unruly family, had neither time nor inclination to pursue the universal truth. Also, her diffidence bordering on shyness concealed a flinty determination that kept her steadfast to views acquired in the last century. The old Indian dhurrie that hung from a downstairs room door to protect us from the winter draughts was never replaced, for its associations with a long dead, much-loved aunt were ever present. Possessions, like beliefs, were not easily relinquished.

One was: just once. As she grew more infirm we had in our care Miss Heaton, the fluttery spinster who had brought the news to my father of his suspected defection to the Kaiser. There was an occasion when her nephew, accompanied by his wife and an unlikeable Pekinese dog, came down from Yorkshire ostensibly to discuss their relative's welfare; but, as my father afterwards remarked, the predatory gleam in their eyes was unmistakable. They landed on us for tea and my mother, who never normally allowed pets in the house, had to endure the Peke's presence snuffling under the tea table. Suddenly its mistress swooped on the slop basin which was already half full of dregs of cold tea, declaring loudly that her little dog simply loved them, and put it on the floor for the excited animal to lap. Throughout the rest of the proceedings my mother maintained a tight-lipped and frosty silence. When her guests had gone she called Kathleen to take the – to her – desecrated slop basin into the yard and smash it up with the coal hammer. She watched stonily as the rose-patterned china bowl was demolished and the fragments consigned to the ash house – that final resting place, as I was all too soon to learn – of things tinged with moral obloquy.

To return to my search for an interlocutor, the prince was trickier. One evening when he came to say goodnight he pulled off the shelf above my head one of the Russian dolls he had given me when I was very small. In those days they were not identical girls wearing a sarafan. A set might start like that but then alternate, boy, girl and so on until the smallest doll would be a baby in swaddling clothes. As the prince shook the dolls out on my bed he barked, with just a touch of exasperation, 'The search for knowledge, Boy, is like peeling an onion. With each layer removed you think you have found the centre. And when you have destroyed the onion you will be left with nothing but your eyes full of tears. Look, Boy, at these silly dolls, how they invite you to penetrate deeper and you arrive' – here he held up the smallest – 'not at the heart of the matter, but with a caricature in miniature of what you started with. And don't go catching on to the current craze that would have us believe that history is progress! That is a mere conceit. History is just one damn' thing after another. If you don't believe me, listen to Belton's lungs heaving when he brings up the coals tomorrow morning.' And with that he crushed his cigar butt in the underside of one of the smaller dolls.

The next best thing to having someone in whom to confide is to have access to a sounding board. Some might even consider it better, for it amplifies and projects the voice without ever answering back. My sounding board was Hogg.

A familiar figure to us all, Hogg plied his cobbler's trade in the little workshop in Church Yard where William Marwood had made his hangman's nooses. Some coils of hemp were reputed still to lie in the dim and dusty recesses of the rafters where Hogg stored his leathers. Short, balding and Pickwickian, Hogg was gentle and kind. I was always glad that his name in Lincolnshire meant 'yearling' or some small beast. His two daughters consequently were known as 'Bunny', whereas elsewhere they might have been nicknamed 'Piggy'. As it happened, they were both fair of face, so much so that in my imagination they rivalled in their beauty Katherine Swynford of Old Bolingbroke, from whom descended the Tudor kings of England. I thought she must have been the most beautiful woman of all time. All this escaped Hogg, who, somewhat to my father's disdain, was preoccupied with storing up treasure in this life at least sufficient to provide handsome dowries for his flaxen-haired, blue-eyed daughters.

I found myself loitering at his shop with increasing frequency on my way home from school, for I had started to use the footbridge that crossed the Waring at the lane end and thus brought me by his work place. I was greeted, 'Nah then, Professor!' which was a pleasant step up – or so I then thought – from 'Josephus', the rather grandiloquent nickname my father had given me because of his own interest in that first-century Jewish soldier–historian.

Hogg stuck to his last in every sense. To see a skilled artisan at work is always fascinating. I loved watching George, the head baker, flipping a cake mixture with an almost languid hand or the farrier rasping the hooves of the great shire horses; but most of all Hogg fitting a leather with his curved knife, his mouth bulging on one side with hobnails and the other cheek with brads. He would spit them out in rapid succession and bang them home, his finger moving away a blink ahead of the hammer's fall. With his mouth full of steel Hogg could not converse. But he could nod – which he did – as I expounded my cosmic concepts. He was the perfect sounding board and a willing, captive audience.

The pursuit of a new, all-embracing theory of being would have faltered and fallen away at an early stage had it not been for two spectacular crashes. Frank was an expert stilt-walker, keeping alive the Gyrwie tradition by which the fenlander moved around the marshes. We could all stilt-walk, but Frank

... an expert
stilt walker

could run, dance and even waltz going up and down stairways. At galas and Sunday school treats he would appear as a ten-foot-high Pierrot with an additional four feet of conical hat. He was as nimble on his ash poles as an acrobat on a tight-rope.

One afternoon in July, Harold, not to be outdone, gave us an exhilarating display, dancing the polka up and down the stone steps of the granary. As we applauded from below he bent low over the balcony rails and invited anyone 'to have a go'. As he leaned against the balustrade the entire wooden structure gave way and down it crashed carrying Harold with it. At the bottom of the steps he lay lifeless and still.

I was terrified. Would there now be no more laughter, or slyly secreted gifts, or teasing, or protection? What would become of Harold's lurid collection of Donald McGill seaside postcards? I must have been bordering on hysterics for all I remember was a sharp box on the ears and hearing the prince saying in a tone I had never heard before: 'Go, fetch a bucket of cold water, Boy. Don't spill a drop, be as quick as you can!' I fled in search of a pail. Meanwhile Harold was gently lifted and, with Tommy, the yardman, sent on ahead, many hands rushed the unconscious youth to the cottage hospital. There he was revived from his concussion, his head bandaged and a broken collar bone set. The prince returned some time later to find me transfixed where Harold had fallen, still standing by my brimming water bucket, not a drop splashed.

'Good,' he exclaimed, 'now pour it on the roses, and let us paddle round to the mill and watch the evening rise.'

It being rainy, the following Sunday we spent in the Moslem and Frank, with due solemnity, produced the Sunday Book. Harold was present, his spirits as irrepressible as ever. After our preliminary drawings of one another, the prince produced a tumbler of water, a penny and half of a discarded Christmas card. Breathing, I noticed, rather heavily through his nose, the prince leaned forward, placed the card on the glass and the coin on the card. He then flicked the card with his finger and the penny fell into the water as its support shot from under.

'This, ladies and gentlemen,' announced the prince, showman style, 'is Newton's third law of motion – in motion. It demonstrates *inertia*. What did your fellow yellow-belly state? All together now: "Things which are not moving do not start moving by themselves." ' With this the prince took my Merryweather fire engine, the one with the turntable and expanding ladder, and shot it across the hearth to stop it suddenly with the poker, whereupon the driver and his tillerman shot forward, head over heels.

'And,' continued the prince, ' "things which are moving do not stop by themselves." ' Picking up the fallen fireman, the prince added, 'it is their inertia that has carried them forward, just as the absence of inertia allowed gravity to pull the penny down.'

We waited, for we sensed that there was something more to

157

come. There was. 'So, when Harold took his purler the other day, it was inertia that carried him forward and gravity that brought him down. Now, we should try and draw the parabola of his fall, it being a combination of gravity and inertia. . . .' His voice faltered and fell away. He had not lost his audience, but he had nearly foregone the five most precious friends he would ever have. We sat in frozen silence. The evening ended earlier than usual. Frank's meticulous drawings never materialized from the marginal sketches he had made in anticipation of recording the evening's deliberations.

This aftermath of Harold's fall led us to a common but unspoken decision that the prince should not be allowed to get away with it. What was more, he did not know everything. He never knew when it was about to rain. I did, because I knew that cows in meadows sit down just before a shower. My offer to enlighten the prince on this particular point was rejected. 'If you can't tell me why your silly cows sit down,' he said testily, 'don't bother just to describe the phenomenon.'

The prince could be unrelenting at times, particularly if supplies of cough medicine ran low when, as the case then was, Belton was laid up with a bad turn. Even though the prince knew he had hurt us, he was still uncontrite. 'What is the point of being a prince if you don't know how far to go too far!' he later said. This was the nearest we ever had by way of an apology. We were not really interested in apologies, however, only revenge, and in the end we got our own back.

Half-closing day in Horncastle was on a Wednesday. On September afternoons we would set off to get blackberries and nuts on the way to Woodhall Spa, where my mother, accompanied by the prince, liked to motor for tea in the pinewoods. Sometimes there would be a string orchestra playing in the tea-garden; the prince said that it reminded him of home, while for my mother it was a rare interval of complete relaxation.

There was something haunting as well as faintly ludicrous about Woodhall. In the late nineteenth century someone digging for lignite in the peat came across an artesian well rich in iodine. Lincolnshire women in my childhood seemed excessively prone to goitre, so a palatable source of iodine must have been welcomed. In 1890 a Bavarian came and planned, and eventually built with local capital (including a modest investment by my Great-uncle, Alfred Dunham) a miniature Baden-Baden – complete with pump room, hotels, tea houses and a splendid golf links. Among the pinewoods and formal gardens the spa sprang up around a street of genteel houses and shops. In the 1900s these gave way to rows of depressing red brick villas which, at the time of my childhood, were inhabited by impoverished widows and over-hearty bankrupt farmers making do but not, alas, making out. As children we sensed this, but we still enjoyed the façade of faded elegance, particularly the toy-sized railway station with its elaborate fretwork and the moss-lined hanging baskets trailing fuchsia almost to the platform upon which passengers had once alighted to be carried in Victoria or waggonette to the waiting hotels.

The tea-garden that my mother liked to visit was a rustic building set in the pinewoods a few yards from the Pump Room. Its architecture seemed to have been derived from an English conception of a Swiss chalet, with robust overtones of a log cabin which would not have been out of place in the Wild West. Perhaps this was also the inspiration for the rather coyly named 'Kinema-in-the-Woods' a one-storey, half-timbered extravaganza adjoining the tea-garden where, after a dainty tea, courting couples would watch from low-slung steamer chairs the latest Hollywood silent movie.

Further on, along an overgrown path in stands of birch and pine, the remains of Ralph Cromwell's hunting tower, a few miles from his massive keep of Tattershall, dominated the desolate peat hags which gave way on all sides to the encircling fens. It was near here, in sight of the forbidding Tower on the Moor, that we set our trap for the prince. While he and my mother savoured the delights of a peaceful hour in the Woodhall tea-garden, we thumbed through my *Scouting for Boys* and found the drawing of a simple 'elephant pit'. Using our bare hands and our stout blackberrying sticks we dug a shallow ditch, fixed a rudimentary trip wire with a piece of thick string that Harold produced from his pocket and stationed Jane as a look-out to warn us of our approaching elders. When she signalled to us that they were coming down the track, having left the car at the junction with the bumpy lane across the moor from the Kinema-in-the-Woods, Frank and Harold tightened the line and sent Muriel off to entice the prince, without my mother, to join us in the bracken. Wreathed in cigar smoke, the prince strode straight forward and, tripping on the string, came a terrible purler. Unfortunately we had underestimated his weight and instead of just landing on the bracken-covered trap he went headlong through the blackberry bushes and collapsed face down in a huge bed of stinging nettles. Only pride was hurt, mainly because Harold, who tended to overdo things, had shouted derisively, 'We have eaten better men than you for breakfast!' At this, I hopped over the bank and found the prince, cigar still intact, covered in nettle rash. I promptly clutched handfuls of young dock leaves and, crunching them up, applied the green juice to the prince's prominent nose, cheeks, forehead and

... came a terrible purler

hands. His recovery was immediate and gratifying. He had not known that docks and nettles invariably grew alongside; the one to neutralize with its alkaline the acid of the other.

How often does one simple answer unlock the mind? In an instant I saw my cosmic system take shape and slip into a complete pattern as neat as the layout of the Hornby train track in the attic at home. Here was the natural harmony of the cosmos that I was seeking: a shattering awareness of the symbiotic character of all life. At home, I shot upstairs and unearthed from my postcard collection a picture of an egret sitting on the head of a rhinoceros, sent me by the colonial cousin from Tanganyika who had named the tortoises Poley and Poley. The egret kept the rhinoceros' hide free from ticks and waxed fat on the proceeds. I then remembered the humble Nile sparrow tolerated by the crocodile who opened its jaws wide to the bird to clean its teeth of gum lice.

My notebooks soon began to fill. A great-aunt long widowed from an apothecary Poucher gave me a specimen case and collecting box. My researches received a fillip when I discovered that Sir Joseph Banks, who had encouraged the development of the canal linking Horncastle with the Witham and the building of the London to Lincoln main road, *and* was chief botanist on Captain Cook's expedition to the South Seas, came from Horncastle. His house, now a butcher's shop, still carries the drum clock with the gridiron, which Muriel had reproduced on her Christmas cake. Banks provided me with inspiration; he had brought thousands of tropical plants back to England. He was also the cause of the collapse of my theory – but that was later.

I started my botanizing close to home, pulling valerian from the garden's river wall where it sprouted in great crimson tufts from the mortar. (This plant with its tranquillizing properties seemed to be a strange one to name after the Roman emperor who had roasted Horncastle's patron saint.) Marshes and ditch bottoms were explored in the canoe, and I discovered by direct experience the diuretic properties of the dandelion, which the French call, with reason, *le pisenlit*. As the summer wore on specimens accumulated in the bottom warehouse. Jars full of

161

strange seeds and berries piled high. This collection became difficult to classify and by the beginning of September had degenerated into a random jumble. At this point I made a discovery that brought me up short and made me realize that things had indeed got out of hand. The trouble was that Banks had collected from Madagascar the periwinkle plant, *Vinca rosea*. The wretched little thing, I learned to my consternation, contained hundreds of alkaloids and was much used in pharmacology. This knowledge was cold comfort, for it meant I was out of the realm of egrets and stinging nettles. It was all too complex and intricate in its design for my divine tapestry and for some time afterwards I felt profoundly dismayed at being caught out so soon by the force of scientific principles. I threw out my collection and turned my thoughts to exploration instead.

Carrots O'Connor was the unwitting instigator of the only long river journey we made in the canoe. He was always badgering me to be allowed to paddle, and it occurred to the prince and me as we made our preparations for this last voyage of the year that a third party would be useful in the portages we would have to make if we were to paddle down the disused canal as far as we could go to Kirkby-on-Bain – beyond which, so Frank had told us, the canal was unnavigable. It turned out that it was unnavigable in several places before we reached Kirkby, being so choked and overgrown with weeds, and it was late afternoon by the time we tied up to a willow tree near the old lock-keeper's cottage. The prince took a swig of cough medicine and we ate our sandwiches. I left Carrots O'Connor to bait his fishing line – the prince was already stretched out under the willow tree with his hat over his face, his head pillowed on his rolled-up Norfolk jacket – and set out alone across the fields to find the ruins of Kirkstead Abbey. We had seen it marked on our map, but how much was left of the ancient abbey we had no idea; it had fallen to me to make the first reconnaissance. I climbed a gate and sat on the top bar and looked around me over the flat fenland, green and gold in the autumn sunshine. Then I saw it – or thought I did – the tower of the abbey chapel, circled and nearly lost to view in a grove of ash and poplar. I jumped down and ran across two fields and over a ditch, and then it was in front of me. But it was not the ruined abbey that I had found; it was a small chapel enclosed with its ancient graveyard in a square of iron railings, the headstones encrusted with moss and ivy and the paths overgrown with weeds and long grass. The trees stood like sentinels at the four corners of the square. A jackdaw flew out of the bell tower as I approached the wicket gate and entered the enclosure.

I went up the path to the great oak door and lifted the latch. The door swung open and I stole inside and up the short, stone-flagged nave to the sanctuary. Through the narrow, lancet windows the late afternoon sun filtered, and dappled the slender columns with lengthening shadows. The clatter of a distant harvest reaper was the only sound breaking the stillness. Standing before the altar I imagined the beautiful Katherine Swynford, she who had once lived a mere bowshot away at Dogdyke, coming to seek peace and restoration in this tranquil place. The little church had an atmosphere of waiting for a presence which had once enjoyed its quiet and its beauty undisturbed. In the silence and stillness I was intently aware that I was no longer alone.

But the moment was fleeting. The evening light had dimmed and I knew that I should leave and join the others by the canal at Kirkby. As I turned to go I caught sight of the effigy of a recumbent knight, carved in marble, his features hidden by his visor, his right hand on the pommel of his sword. Had he too known Katherine Swynford?

I said nothing of my experience as we paddled homewards, but I knew from the prince's covert glances that my silence did not deceive. But the day and the event made his task easier. He suggested gently as he groped in his haversack for the bottle of cough medicine, that pre-occupation with my cosmic theory would only lead to intolerance and a blinkered attitude to life. With my narrow and puritanical background it might be as well to guard against this – rather like taking iodine to ward off goitre. I was not, after all, the only person who had sought an answer to the eternal riddle!

'History abounds in bores who devised global systems' went on the prince. 'That Swiss doctor, what was the name he gave himself? Paracelsus? He was one of them. Three hundred years ago he dramatically unfolded his version of man and the universe as one gigantic chemical compound. He came to a sticky end.' He looked up through the overhanging branches as he tied up the canoe on our return, adding as an after-thought, 'By the way, his middle name was Bombast.'

This was a familiar word in our household. So I abandoned my grand design, no longer made a point of stopping at Hogg's workshop and, with the jettisoning of my now obsolete plant collection, I threw out many of the shibboleths that burdened my childhood. But this could not be accomplished, I thought, without some kind of dramatic confrontation, for I had so far told no one in the family about this transformation in my life.

One day shortly after our river journey I pulled up a great armful of wood-sorrel, or cuckoo bread, from the canal bank. On entering the house covered in the stuff, as if it were Birnam Wood and I one of Malcolm's soldiers, I was met by my mother and Kathleen.

'What's that?' she hissed.

'Shiggy,' I replied stonily. The prince took a puff of his Corona.

'Destroy it, Kathleen, destroy it! I won't have it in the house!' The prince was nonplussed. Not so Kathleen.

'By Goy, Boy, what have you done?' she asked fearfully, as she carried the tainted plants away to the ash house where the raked clinkers and coals from the bake oven were still smouldering as if they were indeed the fires of purgatory waiting for the unrepentant. I knew very well what I had done. 'Shiggy' is the Lincolnshire name for cuckoo bread, forbidden to be touched by the puritans of my county, let alone brought into the house. To them it was redolent of decadence, and with its peculiar pungent smell, of putrefaction and sinful vices. Milk from cows that had eaten shiggy went sour in the butter churn – a sure sign that the Devil had been at work.

It was just as well for me, therefore, that the Great August Horse Fair descended on Horncastle with much bustle and

... a great armful of wood sorrel

excitement, providing a timely and healthy diversion from my Paracelsian search for cosmic order – the physical evidence of which was a pile of unusual additions to Belton's compost heap. Then a dramatic incident at the Fair itself presaged the life I was eventually to lead and gave me a much-needed sense of purpose.

TWELVE

The Best Carpenter

... the disappearance
of Poley and Poley

*T*he well-remembered events of that August began with the disappearance of Poley and Poley. One moment they were gloomily munching their tired lettuce leaves, their outer shells gleaming dully in the afternoon sunshine, and the next – they had vamoosed! I knew they were not on one of their walkabouts across the Market Place; it was too early for them to hibernate; and they could not be in the garden for I had searched in every nook and cranny. Jane, with a forced brightness in her voice that did not deceive me, suggested that as they were amphibians they had taken off down the river, and if they could climb up the water steps they would soon come back, possibly with some young. When, a week later, they had still not returned to their corner of the garden I reconciled myself to their permanent absence. Any sadness I felt was dispelled soon enough, in the manner of childhood, when August arrived.

On Bank Holiday, the first Monday of August, we held our gala and gymkhana. My sisters, being Red Cross volunteers, manned the first aid tent with a Dunham cousin in charge. Frank and Harold gave stilt-walking demonstrations; I ran in sack and three-legged races and gorged on ice cream – not yet encumbered by hygiene laws and therefore rich in flavour. Some years the Stanton Hill Colliery Band, or the band from its neighbouring mine at Creswell in Derbyshire came to play – a reminder of their stay with us during the miners' strike. The gala was followed by the Skegness to Horncastle walking match, a distance of some twenty-five miles. Beginning at Skegness by the Clock Tower on the sea front, the route led across the fens through Burgh-le-Marsh and up into the wolds through Partney and Dunham Hills, ending in a long, fast, downhill finish from Toynton Top to the Market Place in Horncastle. That August, with our encouragement, the one-legged upholsterer entered the event. Much to everyone's amazement he led the field easily, being about a mile ahead when he reached Burgh-le-Marsh. But by the time he got to Partney the blisters caused by the friction of his crutches had flared up under his armpits, and forced him to retire from the race. Alas, there was no longer available St Oswald's earth with which to bring about a miraculous cure.

... he led the field easily

Then, on August the eleventh the Horse Fair burst upon us.
One day the Market Place was sleeping in the sun, with shop
blinds drawn to shade the wares, then the next it and the streets
and yards around would be thick with straw and manure and
every breed and condition of horse. Strings of them, led by
grim-visaged, swarthy men clattered through the town and
were manoeuvred into lines or groups. Gypsy vardos were
encamped along the roadside verges, whence women, bright-
eyed with gold earrings and patterned kerchiefs, made sorties
to sell clothes' pegs or tell fortunes. Urchins darted in and out,
earning a few coppers by holding horses' heads. Farmers,
replete with beer, and horse-copers, full of whisky after deals
were clinched, rolled around the Bull Ring and occasionally
fell into the Bain or the Waring. Public houses during the
Horse Fair, which lasted eleven days, were exempt from
normal licensing hours restrictions. Temporary grog shops
received licenses and were open all day, recognizable by the

holly bush hung over their doorways. Horse fairs are a delight to the brewers and a joy to the distillers, for without them how could any horse ever be bought or sold?

The prince in white buckskin breeches, high-laced boots, buff waistcoat with brass buttons, foulard, Norfolk jacket and broad-brimmed hat would move effortlessly round hunters and cavalry chargers, occasionally looking in a mouth and tapping teeth with his cane. He would talk quietly with the gypsies in their own tongue and always seemed in his element, although he neither bought nor sold horseflesh. In his comings and goings we recognized an air of mystery and preferred almost intuitively to keep it that way. Thus we were free to indulge ourselves in speculation almost to the point of fantasy.

We knew, for instance, that the prince had been brought up on his family's estates in the Crimea, the grounds of which had been laid out and kept by Scottish gardeners, for he sometimes called Belton by the name of MacNab. His family had diplomatic connections in Constantinople and it was there as a young man he had met my Great-uncle Morton. Being childless, the Mortons had taken to the young refugee, and thus it was that after the Bolshevik revolution and service with the White Russian forces and the Imperial Army, the prince made his tortuous way westward across Europe and ended his journey at the Mortons' house at Thimbleby Top. Uncle Morton – Morton Bey to give him his honorary title – had sailed his steam yacht down the Bosphorus for the last time in 1908 and headed home for retirement as Inspector-General of the Ottoman Bank. In due course the Mortons found their way to Thimbleby, where they built a spacious verandahed house with a magnificent view over the wolds towards Scamblesby. They named it 'Moda' after the lovely little Turkish town (now Izmir), where they had lived for so many years.

When they died Uncle and Aunt Morton were buried together in Thimbleby churchyard. Their headstone bore no dates, for Aunt Morton was a trifle vain, even in death, when it came to divulging her age. My mother, who was much attached to them as they were to her, would feel prompted now and then to have flowers put on their grave. She always sat in

... occasionally looking in a mouth and tapping teeth

the car at the gate while some member of the family executed her commission. From this my father would be exempt, lest his discretion be unequal to suppressing his mirth, for the Mortons' headstone bore on it this confident, if incorrectly attributed, statement:

I HOPE TO SEE MY PILOT FACE TO FACE

WHEN I HAVE CROST THE BAR.

THE DAISY *(1847)*

When the prince first came to England he stayed some months at Thimbleby with his old friends, but either because of their age and infirmity or possibly because Aunt Morton became apprehensive at the amount of cough medicine consumed by her husband and his guest, the prince then moved down to Horncastle and made his summer home with us. Thereafter his annual visits went uninterrupted, except for the year he spent with Great-uncle Tommy Dunham at Ashby Puerorum.

Tommy, the 'ickeny' Dunham, was Aunt Morton's youngest brother and a confirmed bachelor. Unheralded visitors were not made welcome, particularly if they were ladies. The reason for this was the presence of his grandfather clock which stood in an alcove leading from the parlour into the gunroom. Above the brass face of the clock was a delicately enamelled painting of the Garden of Eden. The Tree of Life grew in the centre with the serpent entwined in its branches and in the foreground Adam and Eve, naked. As the hour chimed, Eve swivelled and raised her hand to the apple. Adam also swung forward and placed his hand upon her breast. This lascivious sight was considered unsuitable for ladies and before they were admitted a lace table runner, kept for this purpose, was draped over the clock face. Nevertheless, although we rarely visited Uncle Tommy, we saw the prince daily when he and Uncle Tommy motored in to park the De Dion Bouton in our yard, with Uncle Tommy's parrot hanging in its cage from the back of the car. One hot day when he had come to see my mother he left the car engine running and the unfortunate parrot expired from the exhaust fumes. Uncle Tommy mourned its death extravagantly, and because it had happened in our yard held us responsible. His visits ceased for a time and the prince came back to us.

If we ever complained about our summer guest, my mother would say, 'Now children, remember this is the only real home he has.' Where was he then, when absent throughout the year? Judging by the presents he brought us, he was clearly much travelled, but whatever else he did and wherever else he went he never missed the Horncastle Horse Fair. Although it was not the event it had been in the nineteenth and early part of the twentieth centuries it was still the largest fair of its kind in England and buyers came from as far afield as the United States and the Argentine.

That August, the year the tortoises disappeared, I with other small fry was darting in and out of a string of ponies in the Bull Ring when a powerful hand locked on my wrist. I looked up and saw a lean, black-haired gypsy glaring at me. I was startled, but not afraid, for I had seen him earlier in the day going into the Saracen's Head with the prince. He indicated to me that I should hold the halters of a pair of cobs while he went about some business.

He was gone, it seemed, for a very long time, and the horses became restless. I did not dare to walk them as I would be sure to lose their places in the line of horses, rumps to the pavement, that stretched across the Waring and beyond. Slithering on the dung-coated straw I hung on, emitting grown-up growls of 'Nah, then!' 'Aye-up!' and 'Woaha then!' and was just about to lose control of their heads when a hand took the halters from me. It was the prince who had returned with the horse coper. The gypsy suddenly grabbed my hair in both hands (my cap had fallen under the horses' hooves), whistled softly and muttered something in Romany.

'What did he say?' I asked the prince.

'He says, Boy, that you will have a long and fortunate life.'

'By Goy! What else did he say?'

'That you have a double crown.'

'What about it, then?'

'He says that you will go away and earn your bread in a foreign land.'

'Gaarh!' I shouted, as if I was still trying to quieten the cobs.

With the gypsy's fingers still clutching my hair I felt an electric current had slammed into me. I tore myself free and sprinted away wildly as if the Furies were on my tail, desperate to find Harold and seek his protection. I thought he would be up on the Wong, stuffing himself with the jellied eels the Romanies cooked and sold at their encampment. Carrots O'Connor saw me as I ran round the Bull Ring. He too had been earning a few coppers holding horses' heads, but he dropped them when he saw me and loped alongside, looking at me anxiously as he sensed that something was amiss. Sirdar Smith saw me as he was standing in his grandmother's doorway and ran out to join us.

. . . suddenly grabbed my hair in both hands

Harold was nowhere to be found on the Wong so I continued to run, less aimlessly now, past the Baptist Chapel, down Cagthorpe and across the Waring, into St Mary's churchyard and across the corner of the Market Place to sink exhausted on the granary steps. My fellow members of the Foreign Legion stared at me as I told them what had happened. They were not disbelieving, for even as repeated by me the prophecy carried an air of dread certainty. It was not that it was unwelcome, but it was very startling. Apart from short journeys in the George Marina, or wrapped up in the Maud in the pony trap, I had never gone farther from home than Lincoln. I had never travelled on a bus, tram or train – but I *had* seen an aeroplane once when a Gloster Gladiator from Cranwell had made a forced landing in the field behind Uncle Tommy's house at Ashby Puerorum.

The prince in his wanderings, and colonial cousins and missionaries on furlough had brought the world to us; none of us had felt the need to go out into it, particularly when we saw the readiness with which they were absorbed into our private domain. But now the gypsy's forewarning had made me suddenly aware of a future awaiting me beyond the charmed circle. I did not yet know how I was going to cross the boundaries of my imagination, for I realized, even then, that travel was much more than just a matter of going from place to place. The crackle of morse from ships at sea picked up of an evening on Frank's discarded crystal set, for example, transported me further in my mind than did the journeys of wicked Uncle Jack to his home in the Canadian Rockies.

The modest excursions that my Foreign Legion friends and I made now assumed an added significance as we began to prospect the highways and byways that lay beyond our immediate confines. Up to that time we had always used, while going about our daily business and in order to avoid our elders' admonitory gaze, the lanes, tracks over stiles, the towpath along the waterside and in Horncastle itself, the narrow entries between streets – but whichever way we took it always led us back home. Now we went further afield and discovered for the first time the wide, grassy 'swaths' or drovers' roads which ran for long stretches over the wold tops and across the bottoms. We pronounced them 'waths' with the traditional flat 'a'. These mysterious pathways or grassy lanes, which followed the contours and were bordered on either side by high, hawthorn hedges, had been made over the centuries by drovers driving cattle or sheep to market, connecting the northern wolds with centres of population like Lincoln, Grantham and the port of Boston. The width of the swath was the approximate size of a small flock of sheep, that is, about twenty sheep could graze alongside one another as they made their slow way over the hills. No longer in use, the swaths nevertheless retained an air of long forgotten spirits of an ancient people, and none of us would have liked to walk them alone. Sometimes we would come across a group of gypsy vardos with their horses tethered, and once in the darkening mist of a winter afternoon we were passed by the mud-spattered figure of our local huntsman, like some ghostly horseman, leading his hounds back to the kennels at West Ashby.

Experiences such as these were later to be translated more prosaically in another direction when we turned our attention to the exploration of the railway line, on which at least I had yet to travel. A seven-mile spur of single track, it began at Horncastle and joined our town at Kirkstead to the main line. An 'ickeny' station, the one platform ended in ramps, not steps, and as these fell beneath the overhang of the platform roof they were always slippery with moss and a hazard to the unwary. The station boasted a goods siding, but the goods sheds had been built on the opposite side at a right angle to the terminal roads. This called for a turntable and a track that on the level cut across the passenger line. An elderly dray horse trundled the wagons one by one round the turntable and over the line to the sheds. To top the lot, the signals gantry, instead of clanking up and down or being of the rare somersault variety spun round wildly as if trying to semaphore with one arm.

Woodhall was the only other station on the line before reaching Kirkstead junction. Rambler roses tumbled over the railings, it had elegant fret-worked buildings and twin plat-forms, one of which even boasted a bookstall. But after this decorous interval the 'ickeny' side surfaced again when the line reached the junction. It had been built facing the wrong way, so when the Horncastle local pulled in it had to steam down the line for perhaps a hundred yards before it could be shunted back into its siding at the station. The same procedure was followed on returning. Down the main line went the local: it stopped, the points were switched, and the engine pulled our little train backwards all the way along the spur to home.

Nevertheless, ours was a profitable railway. Its engines were painted the livery colour of Lincoln green. Our carriages – if ancient – were solidly built of mahogany and lined with walnut. Three times a week a carriage with a first-class compartment formed part of the through train to Boston, where it would be hooked up to the London express. On this train the Reverend Isaacs travelled every Monday morning en route for the British Museum to seek refuge from his parochial duties.

Happily, when the Great Northern Railway merged to form the London and Northeastern Railway little changed. Known affectionately as the 'Late and Never Early Railway', the LNER never acquired the self-important bustling air of the Great Western or the London, Midland and Scottish. Even under the new management the engine driver still gave an extra toot on his locomotive whistle should a regular passenger be late. And if that did not bring him running our one porter was sent on his bicycle to rouse him.

The delights of railway travel were soon to come to me, but for the moment they remained in toyland. My frequent visits to the station yard were solely for checking details of layout and rolling stock – to be faithfully reproduced on the attic floor with my increasingly elaborate Hornby train sets. In the end it was to the rivers and the canal that ran by our house that the would-be journeying boy returned. Not that the rivers were navigable any more: far from it. By the time I was born the Dunham barge traffic had all pretty well been transferred to the railway and the canal was thick with weed and almost impenetrable. Few of the locks worked and only a skilled canoeist strong enough to make frequent portages could navigate. No longer could one even skate down it as my mother and her family's maid had done in the Great Frost of 1895, carrying baskets of food to her grandfather's shivering boatmen locked in the ice on their frozen barges.

It was about this time that I became much attracted by the exploits of Captain John Smith who had been born in the sixteenth century at Willoughby, across the wolds from Partney, and had been an apprentice shipwright in Boston. Here was someone I could emulate. I too would build a boat and sail uncharted seas as he had done. I was not clear how I would do this, for I had no skills and for the moment no means of acquiring them, but with the optimism of youth I thought something would turn up, and eventually it did. My father had recently bought for half-a-crown each a dozen or so car-penter's benches with a metal vice at one end and a wooden one at the other and was intending to use them for stacking supplies in the lower warehouse where the flagstones were always damp.

With my new-found ambition I viewed the familiar contents of warehouse and granary with a fresh eye as I helped to pile up the tea chests from Ceylon or Tientsin, sacks of sultanas from Morocco and dates from Tangier, tins of corned beef from Montevideo, Dutch cheeses, Jamaican bananas and sugar from distant Demarara. When the work was completed it was found that there was one extra carpenter's bench. I asked my brothers to set it up for me under the window overlooking the water steps; there was wood a-plenty from the emptied chests, crates and boxes, and Frank found me some discarded wood-working tools. The acquisition of skills was more difficult, but not insuperable. Mr Turner, the Methodist undertaker, had a joiner's yard and his two sons were whistling friends of my brothers. He was a kindly man and I knew that I could run round to his workshop any day after school and watch as his carpenters effortlessly plied plane, chisel or saw, turning out chairs, chests, cupboards and coffins from a wide variety of woods and veneers using rule of thumb and without benefit of plan or blueprint.

After a few days of this I ended my passive apprenticeship and returned to the bottom warehouse knowing exactly what to do – which was to reproduce the correct working environment. I selected a number of quite long planks from some dismantled crates, preserving the nails and screws very carefully, for I had none. I clamped one of the planks upright in the wooden vice, shaving it down with a long wooden plane. It made a singing, granular hiss as it swept along the wood – pine being an easy wood to handle. In no time at all, I stood blistered but happy, ankle deep in sweet-smelling wood shavings. But the next evening, when I returned to work, I found a card pinned to the window sill above my bench and on it, written in my father's faultless copperplate were the puzzling words:

THE BEST CARPENTER DOES NOT

MAKE THE MOST CHIPS

"Westward Ho" I shouted, as we paddled resolutely towards the east

The planks I had left stacked against the wall were no longer there and the jam jars in which I had carefully hoarded nails and screws were empty. The tools I had left scattered about the bench had been hung from improvised racks. It was clear that someone had been hard at work while I had been at school all day.

Some instinct prompted me to run to the water steps. I expected to see the canoe in its place at the stanchion but it was no longer there, tugging gently in the downstream current from its mooring ring. Instead, a huge raft rode high in the water at the end of a long painter. Four empty barrels of the kind used for storing molasses had been resealed to provide buoyancy. These were lashed with thick hemp from the orange boxes to a deck assembled from my planks, and from an oblong hole in the middle protruded a long ash punting pole with an iron flange at the tip. This later turned out to be a discarded bakehouse peel that George had offered as his contribution to the exercise.

My brothers had surpassed themselves. I could not deny that their shipbuilding skills were vastly superior to mine, and all feelings of annoyance quickly disappeared. They had made it to carry at least four and although it rode high in the water it could not be capsized. It was greeted with delight by my mates in the Foreign Legion for up to that time only Carrots O'Connor had been allowed in the canoe, and here was a vessel fit for a whole crew. As I stepped on to the raft for the first voyage I had visions of high adventure and exploration of lands unknown.

The Foreign Legion turned out in force, armed with home-made paddles to supplement the punting pole. Ostensibly the object of this initial journey was to find, rescue and bring home in triumph the wandering tortoises; but they were soon forgotten, and by the time we had cleared the bridge and left the bemused land-bound anglers behind we knew we were in the wake of Captain John Smith. 'Westward ho!' I shouted as we paddled resolutely towards the east.

... Nothing I prefer more on a Sunday morning than three Xmas

1 935, the year after I acquired the raft, brought a fundamental change in my life: I went away to school. This decision on the part of my parents which was to have such a radical effect on my future was taken as the result of an accumulation of events, insignificant at the time, even trivial. But who can tell from what small beginnings may be derived the ordering of our existence?

An enormous billboard appeared on the Dunham Hills in one of my Uncle Arthur's fields to catch the eye of travellers on the main road to Skegness. The display of such hoardings was still a rare feature in our rural landscape and would certainly not go unremarked. The poster showed a benign-looking, white-haired clergyman in his cassock sitting snug in his book-lined study, writing what must have been his weekly sermon. He sat with his pen poised in one hand and a large briar pipe clasped in the other. The caption read:

Nothing I prefer more on a Sunday morning

than THREE NUNS!

Cresting the hill, father would accelerate the car, or whip up the pony if we were in the governess cart, throw back his head and roar with laughter. The poster brought his mild anti-clericalism and intense dislike of the smoking habit nicely into one focus. At my tender age, of course, the joke was lost on me. But the youngest must never be out-done, and I joined my father in his mirth by laughing immoderately on one occasion, which caused him to glance at me rather sharply. Perhaps if the advertisement had been for Baby's Bottom, or Parson's Pleasure, or any other oddly named pipe tobacco, I might have seen the humour in what I *felt* should make me laugh – but not enjoying three nuns on a Sunday morning.

In some indefinable way, however, my interest in the wider world was quickening. That June, by which time the prince had arrived, the League of Nations Association held a peace ballot – designed to test British support for the League, and my sisters participated in the canvass. My father chaired a meeting in the Corn Exchange to which we all went. In the event it was agreed to support collective resistance to armed aggression – if other members of the League acted similarly; but then everything was turned upside down when Italy was allowed to get away with her conquest of Abyssinia.

I began to be aware, too, of my rapid physical growth, for I had some difficulty in wriggling down the cellar tunnel to eavesdrop on my father and the prince when pushed down, like Belton's ferret, by my brothers. But I was in time to hear the prince say, 'Francis, if we let Mussolini grab Abyssinia, it will mean war. Not this year or next; but eventually we shall have to fight Germany again and, this time, Italy too.' I duly reported on this to Frank and Harold and together we repaired to the Moslem to look for an atlas. I had difficulty in reaching for it as the library steps were always removed to the prince's room when we came to stay. Two of the steps were hinged, revealing box-like compartments, in one of which was kept a chamber-pot. The prince always put the steps by his bedroom fireplace, filled the pot with water and stored his cigars in the top compartment, thus contriving a makeshift but highly effective humidor.

We found Abyssinia in the atlas and asked our father for a book about the country. But the only one he could offer was Doctor Johnson's *Rasselas*. Not the best briefing perhaps, but it serves to demonstrate the somewhat eclectic nature of his library, which was almost entirely composed of purchases at vicarage auctions. (A year later, when the Spanish Civil War broke out, the one relevant work we could find was George Borrow's *A Bible in Spain*. When I complained, I was advised that the discerning reader could find in it ample explanation for the cause of civil strife in that country.)

Not only was the world beyond the frontiers of our everyday experience changing, but so was the more intimate and immediate one of our family – the first sign of which had surfaced three years earlier on the execution of Mrs Winters. Tennis parties from which I was excluded claimed my brothers and sisters. Muriel rode a lot and Jane had become fleet of foot in sporting events and swam a mile, to everyone's consternation. Frank and Harold disappeared for long summer evenings with girls in long summer dresses. My father and the prince were much occupied with the small estate bequeathed to my mother. Our colonial cousin on leave from Tanganyika had chosen to go shooting at Bisley rather than spend his time with us. I hankered after being part of their world – which had up to then had not seemed desirable. But then Ethel, the new kitchenmaid, arrived.

I was acutely aware of her, with breasts like small apples and heavy hips. She moved slowly, almost dreamily. Her presence in some inexplicable way disturbed me. Her dark Titian coloured hair was very typical of the country girls in whom Norse and Danish blood still ran. Her body smell entranced me.

Whether some jocular remark to Uncle Arthur was respons-ible for the change in the poster on the hoarding, or the lease of it by the tobacco company expired I never knew. But early in the summer the advertisement was changed to one promoting BP petrol. This time it portrayed a young man in a snappy red sports car with his long muffler precariously flying in the slip stream, and a blissful, idiotic grin on his face. His features uncannily resembled those of my brother Frank. The caption read:

A motorist's paradise – FLAT OUT ON ETHYL.

The coincidences were too much to prevent the obvious joke: 'What is Frank's definition of a motorist's paradise?' – to which the answer, of course, was 'Flat out on Ethel'. Happily, Ethel remained in total ignorance. So did I; but it did not prevent me from repeating the joke in order to ingratiate myself with my elders in the hope that I would be included in their inexplicable comings and goings. To no avail: all I achieved was a show of irritation and even more distant exclusion. This loud repetition of jokes which I did not understand, followed by shouts of incomprehending laughter, would have had no serious repercussion had it not been for the one that my brothers considered 'the giddy limit', as they put it.

That summer of 1935 we had celebrated King George's

Silver Jubilee with bunting in the streets and bonfires on the hilltops. Each schoolchild had received a jubilee mug with a new copper penny nestling inside. 'Good for boiling cabbage,' was my father's comment to my mother, who thought he sometimes harboured republican sentiments – although on this occasion she had no cause to complain in view of the amount of flags and bunting we strung across the street. Then the Prince of Wales, that wayward darling of the Empire, had fallen in love with a lady from Baltimore. Unfortunately she was not only a commoner but also already married. This relationship between the Prince of Wales and Mrs Simpson was at first withheld from the British public, but our prince whose mysterious errands took him to the continent was better informed from reading the French newspapers – as always, dogged in their devoted attention to details of our Royal

*... early in the summer
the advertisement was changed*

Family's private lives. From my vantage point in the cellar I listened to the prince gossiping to my father about the possible implications of the scandal, and overnight became something of an authority on the subject – or so I thought. It transpired that Mrs Simpson was to be granted a divorce. While this was taking place she was to live quietly in a villa in the south of France. This gave rise to a ribald conundrum amongst the knowledgeable:

'Why does the Prince of Wales carry a tin opener on his watch chain?'

'Why?'

'Because Mrs Simpson keeps her cunt in Cannes!'

I had no idea where Cannes was. Nor what a cunt was, but my rushing up to my elders and posing this joke, inexplicable to me but offensive to them, was the final straw.

With ears cuffed and backside booted I was sent home in disgrace and placed in Coventry. The sanctity of the attic playroom offered no solace as I kicked gloomily at the wainscot and considered the latest news – that Kathleen had announced that morning she was leaving to marry a postman. My world had come to a stop.

That evening I wriggled for the last time into the cellar tunnel and heard the prince say to my father: 'Boy should go away to school, Francis. His brothers' lives are here in Horncastle but his will eventually take him away. There are excellent Quaker boarding schools and you should seek a place for him in one.'

'Spider' Birkett, clerk of Lincoln Meeting was summoned and together he and my father visited several Friends' schools. They finally decided on one in the distant Cotswolds that had been founded for the sons and daughters of Quakers who, like my father, had 'married out'; that is, had married non-Friends and thus, in those days, had been 'read out' of their Meetings. By being educated in such a school its founders hoped that the children of those who had so erred would be readmitted to the Society.

To be educated 'in the manner of Friends', to use a Quaker expression, did not contain too many surprises for me, brought up as I was in a Quaker household. I had already accompanied my father to Meetings at Lincoln and once to a

... wriggled for the last time into the cellar tunnel

gathering of Friends at Brant Broughton, but I knew no one who had gone away to school, whether Quaker or not. I found myself curiously resigned to an enterprise not exactly of my own choosing, although I saw it as the first step in the fulfilment of the gypsy's forewarning.

On the Sunday before leaving on this new adventure the prince and I were up on Keal Hill with others of the family. It was the end of harvest and the fields were full of short stubble. A cock pheasant rose into the air with a whirr of its wings as we walked to the top of the wold and looked out over the fens towards Boston, the Stump a dark sentinel against the evening sky. The time for evensong approached and then suddenly the deep boom of the great bell came to us on the south wind. The change-ringers swept into a seemingly endless series of peals, making the air vibrate even at a distance until, just before six o'clock their clamour died away leaving, for the final minute, the faint, almost tinny sound of the tenor bell picking its way across the fens towards us. There was no 'Brides of Enderby' that night, but the warning peal was not unheeded; for, in the stillness that followed, its very silence brought an awareness of hazards yet unknown.

The next morning Jane and Muriel said goodbye with that abstracted air they assumed when some prank was on foot. Harold thumped me on the back with a knowing smile. In the yard Tommy was rubbing down the George Marina as if it was a horse. 'Nah then, Boy!' he said by way of hail and farewell. I was putting the last of my boxes into the car when there was a great clatter over the cobbles and into the yard came Uncle Tommy Dunham in the De Dion with his gamekeeper in the back seat. To the amazement of all present Uncle Tommy came over and pressed a florin into my hand. He just as quickly departed, the gamekeeper revealing his few remaining teeth in a grimace that could have been taken for a smile.

It was time to be off, for I saw beyond the rookery behind the Belton's cottage the puff of steam from the engine four seconds before I heard its whistle. Once in the compartment I lowered the window by pulling on the huge leather strap. Frank waved from the car. My mother stood on the platform

like a Roman matron unmoving, but not unmoved. It being Monday, the Reverend Isaacs was securely ensconced in a corner seat with his back to the engine, reading *The Times*. I had already said my farewells to my father and been presented with a wristwatch – and a reminder not to forget to wind it. Of the prince there was no sign. There was another shriek from the engine whistle and, with a clang of buffers the train began hoarsely to puff its way along the single track that ran parallel with the weed-choked canal. It bumped over the turntable, past the goods shed on the left and the water crane with its hose swinging and dripping like an elephant's trunk. I waved to the signalman in the signal box and then, as the train gathered speed, rattling over the points under the signal gantry there was a series of sudden, violent explosions. My brothers had persuaded the platelayer to put fog signals on the line. These percussion caps gave off thunderous warning bangs when the locomotive rolled over them, and as they sounded off in the

... into the yard came Uncle Tommy Dunham in the De Dion

still, morning air I knew for sure that I was on my way to the
Great Game of Life. The Reverend Isaacs appeared not to have
noticed anything untoward; he simply rose and pulled on the
strap to close the compartment window.

Above my head in the luggage rack was the bag the prince
had given me the evening before. We had been sitting in the
garden, he in the rattan chair. 'Always be properly turned out,'
he said, in a matter-of-fact way. Then flicking his cigar stump
over the roses to expire with a hiss in the river, he reached
under the chair and produced an oblong leather and canvas
holdall. It was a fencing bag he had bought for me in Paris as a
parting present, copious enough to contain all the fencing gear
I had. But then he slid it back under the seat. 'For tomorrow,'
he said. I thanked him awkwardly, not knowing what to say.
He touched my arm lightly in a dismissive gesture.

There was just a breath of autumn in the air. The light was
fading under the sycamore. There was little time left.

...there was a series of sudden, violent explosions

'Come on!' the prince said rising from the rattan chair, tugging his glove tight and buttoning up the neck of his jacket. We saluted one another gravely.

'On guard!' He stepped forward, raising his foil and with the familiar flick of the hand tapped his mask into place.

'Good, advance!' I feinted to draw his blade. We fenced cautiously for a minute. I disengaged and lunged. He parried my attack and flicked out a riposte. I tapped his blade and went for his flank, risking a long, low lunge on to the slippery grass.

'Splendid!' exclaimed the prince as he helped me to my feet. 'But write, dear Boy, write always with grace . . . elegantly.' Then, after a moment during which I was allowed to collect myself, 'on guard, now this time more discipline and control!' Our blades crossed.

I thought I saw the prince smile through his mask.

... I thought I saw the prince smile through his mask.